C000005109

OFFICIAL
ENGLAND
WORLD CUP 2006
PREVIEW GUIDE

OFFICIAL
ENGLAND

WORLD CUP 2006
PREVIEW GUIDE

Tim Hill

HarperSport
An Imprint of HarperCollinsPublishers

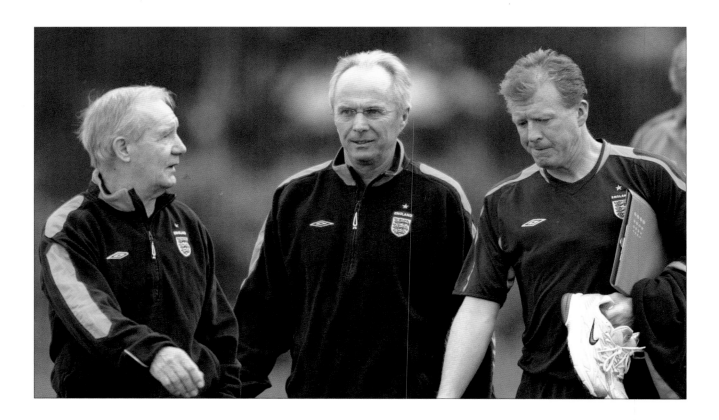

First published in paperback in 2006 by
HarperSport
an imprint of HarperCollins
London

TheFA.com

2

© The Football Association Ltd 2006

The FA Crest and FA England Crest are official trademarks
of The Football Association Ltd and are the subject of extensive
trademark registrations worldwide

The views expressed in this publication are not necessarily those of The FA or any of its affiliates

All rights reserved. No part of this publication may be reproduced,
stored in a retrieval system, or transmitted, in any form or by any means, electronic, mechanical,
photocopying, recording or otherwise, without the prior written permission of the publishers

The Author asserts the moral right to be identified as the author of this work

A CIP catalogue record for this book is available from the British Library

Produced by Atlantic Publishing
Photography © Empics

All information within this book correct at time of printing, March 2006

ISBN-13 978-0-00-721694-9
ISBN-10 0-00-721694-7

Printed and bound in Great Britain by Butler & Tanner, Frome

The HarperCollins website address is www.harpercollins.co.uk

Contents

England's Path to the Finals 8

The Groups 42

A word from Sven

Welcome to The FA's Official England World Cup Preview Guide – a World Cup year that we hope will give us some fantastic memories.

This is my third international tournament as England Head Coach, and I feel that we are stronger now than we have ever been in the last five years. Never before have we been able to call on so many world-class players. We have skill, energy and experience.

I am confident, and so are my players, that we can go into a match against any team in the world without fear. We are good enough to go all the way.

So, on behalf of all the squad, thank you for supporting the England team.

Sven-Göran Eriksson

England's Path to the Finals

Aspiring to be the best

England should reach the final. At least, they ought to according to FIFA's seeding system. The bookies won't have Sven's side as second favourites, but the No. 2 berth is where England emerged following the application of FIFA's formula, a combination of performance at the last two World Cups – with greater weighting placed on Japan and Korea – and world ranking over the past three years.

When the draw was made, England was actually ranked ninth, which, to all but the most blinkered patriot, is probably a more accurate reflection of the standing of a team that has reached the quarter-finals of the last two major tournaments. But as Greece proved at Euro 2004, any team can live the dream; all it has to do is go on a seven-match winning streak. Maybe even five victories would be enough. The present England side is more than capable of doing that, but there are probably 10 other countries whose fans will believe exactly the same, with the remaining 22 crossing fingers and avoiding ladders.

Just five dropped points in a 10-match qualifying series was a highly creditable performance – only Holland bettered that in the Euro zone. The hiccups came at unexpected moments. In the opening round, England were held to a 2–2 draw in Austria, after Lampard and Gerrard had given the team a comfortable two-goal cushion. But the low point was undoubtedly last autumn, when England travelled to Windsor Park. The meeting with Northern Ireland came hard on the heels of an abysmal performance in Copenhagen, where the team was thumped 4–1 by Denmark, the country Sven's side had dispatched with such aplomb in the second round in Japan and Korea. That was just a friendly; surely there would be no slip-ups against Lawrie Sanchez's side, ranked 116 in the world? In the event, the mouse roared. David Healy scored the only goal of the match to inflict England's first defeat in a qualifier during the Eriksson era, and the first loss against Northern Ireland since Terry Neill stabbed the only goal of the game at Wembley in the 1972 Home International Championship.

Below: The England team pose before their qualifier against Wales at the Millennium Stadium.
Opposite: Frank Lampard celebrates his goal with David Beckham during the World Cup qualifying match against Austria at Old Trafford.

Reaching the finals for the ninth time

If the result in Belfast was bad enough, it was made worse by a formation that seemed to bewilder the players as much as the onlookers. There were the inevitable calls for Eriksson's head, but the England coach vowed to fight on, win the last two matches and qualify for Germany as group winners.

And so it turned out. England got back on track with a stuttering 1–0 win over Austria at Old Trafford, Frank Lampard converting from the spot in a game most noteworthy for the red card shown to David Beckham, who became the first player to be sent off twice while wearing an England shirt. Other results meant that the team's place in the finals was now assured, and Eriksson duly delivered top spot in Group Six with a 2–1 win over Poland at Old Trafford. Goals from Owen and Lampard gave England the double over their closest rivals. England had reached the finals for the 12th time since making its debut in Brazil in 1950; Germany '74, Argentina '78 and USA '94 are still the only World Cup blanks England has drawn in the past 56 years.

Below: John Terry and Northern Ireland's David Healy battle for the ball during their World Cup qualifier.
Opposite: Joe Cole is challenged by Poland's Radoslaw Sobolewski.

	P	W	D	L	F	A	PTS
ENGLAND	10	8	1	1	17	5	25
POLAND	10	8	0	2	27	9	24
AUSTRIA	10	4	3	3	15	12	15
NORTHERN IRELAND	10	2	3	5	10	18	9
WALES	10	2	2	6	10	15	8
AZERBAIJAN	10	0	3	7	1	21	3

RESULTS:

AUSTRIA 2-2 ENGLAND	ENGLAND 2-0 AZERBAIJAN
POLAND 1-2 ENGLAND	WALES 0-1 ENGLAND
ENGLAND 2-0 WALES	NORTHERN IRELAND 1-0 ENGLAND
AZERBAIJAN 0-1 ENGLAND	ENGLAND 1-0 AUSTRIA
ENGLAND 4-0 NORTHERN IRELAND	ENGLAND 2-1 POLAND

DAVID BECKHAM ENGLAND

Vital cog in an all-star side

Many sportsmen transcend their area of expertise and gain celebrity in different fields, but that description hardly does justice to the iconic status achieved by David Beckham. Arguably the biggest name in world soccer, Beckham is a premium brand as well as an outstanding footballer.

Style guru he may be, yet Becks has never lost sight of the fact that image counts for nothing on the pitch. His tour de force performance against Greece in October 2001, including the last-ditch free-kick which secured England's place at the last World Cup, will live long in the memory.

Beckham first appeared in a United shirt in 1992, though he didn't become a fixture in the side until 1995. He helped United win the double that season, and at the start of his second campaign he left spectators, TV viewers, pundits – and Wimbledon 'keeper Neil Sullivan – all mesmerised with a shot from inside his own half that sailed into the net. It showed the vision and ball-striking technique which would be the hallmarks of his game.

Beckham won his first cap in 1996, under Glenn Hoddle, and went to France '98 as one of young stars of the team. He was vilified for the red card against Argentina in the second round, awarded for a petulant kick at Diego Simeone. Beckham toughed it out and did his talking on the pitch. The rehabilitation was amazing: zero to hero writ large.

Beckham was part of the glorious treble-winning side of 1999 – the year he married former Spice Girl Victoria Adams – but his relationship with Sir Alex Ferguson gradually deteriorated, culminating in a move to Real Madrid in 2003. In the past three years he has flourished in La Liga, becoming a vital cog in an all-star side where competition for places is fierce.

Despite the many footballing highs, the World Cup has not been kind to Beckham. Four years after the 1998 nightmare, Becks went to Japan and Korea carrying a foot injury. He wasn't fully fit in England's run to the last eight, though he at least was able to lay the Argentina ghost to rest by scoring the winner from the spot against the South American side in the group stage. Germany may be his last shot at international football's greatest prize, and Beckham will want to finally show his best form on the biggest stage.

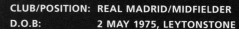

CLUB/POSITION:	REAL MADRID/MIDFIELDER
D.O.B:	2 MAY 1975, LEYTONSTONE
DEBUT:	v MOLDOVA, 1 SEPT 1996
CAPS/GOALS:	87/16

WAYNE ROONEY ENGLAND

Hottest property in world soccer

All World Cup-winning sides have had a special player, one who elevates a team from world class to world beaters. Ronaldo, Zidane, Maradona, Muller, Pele....some of the game's greatest luminaries have taken the tournament by the scruff of the neck. Many place the precociously gifted Wayne Rooney in that bracket.

Rooney was already being hailed as the hottest young property in English football before his wonder strike for Everton against Arsenal in October 2002. Arsene Wenger acclaimed the 16-year-old as the greatest talent he had seen since arriving in England.

Rooney had already netted in a Worthington Cup tie to take over from the legendary Tommy Lawton as Everton's youngest ever marksman; the goal against the Gunners made him the youngest scorer in Premiership history, and the records continued to tumble.

Just four months later Sven made Rooney England's youngest international – 17 years 111 days – when he came off the bench at Upton Park in a friendly against Australia. The game ended in a 3–1 defeat, though in 45 minutes he showed all the hallmarks of an international-class player.

Rooney opened his account in his sixth outing in an England shirt, against Macedonia in a Euro 2004 qualifier in September 2003. His equaliser lifted the side, and England went on to win 2–1. At 17 years 317 days, he had beaten Michael Owen's record as England's youngest marksman.

Rooney went on to become the European Championship's youngest ever goalscorer, albeit briefly, when he netted the first of his brace in the 3–0 win over Switzerland. He hit two more against Croatia, and had he not limped out early in the quarter-final against Portugal, England might not have been packing their bags. Eriksson was among those who equated his impact on the tournament with that made by 17-year-old Pele at the 1958 World Cup.

That summer it became increasingly clear that Everton would struggle to keep the jewel unearthed by scout Bob Pendleton nine years earlier. Manchester United won the race for 'Roonaldo's' signature, and he marked his Old Trafford debut with a sensational hat-trick, in a Champions League tie against Fenerbahce. United ended the season empty-handed, but Rooney's many sparkling displays earned him the PFA Young Player of the Year award.

Rooney's superb strike in the 3–2 win over Argentina last November was his 11th in 28 outings in an England shirt. His volatile temper has been his Achilles' heel. If he can keep that in check, 20-year-old Rooney is surely the ace in Eriksson's pack.

CLUB/POSITION:	MANCHESTER UNITED/STRIKER
D.O.B:	24 OCTOBER 1985, LIVERPOOL
DEBUT:	v AUSTRALIA, 12 FEBRUARY 2003
CAPS/GOALS:	29/11

ENGLAND

PETER CROUCH ENGLAND

Aerial threat and deftness of touch

What a year it's been for Peter Crouch. His goals couldn't save Southampton from the drop in 2004–05, but they did earn him a £7 million move to Liverpool. Rafa Benitez's decision came into sharp focus when Anfield legend Michael Owen found himself surplus to requirements at Real Madrid and expressed a desire to return to his footballing roots. Owen went for more than double Crouch's fee to St James' Park, and was soon off the mark; Crouch was playing well but couldn't find the net. The drought lasted for 21 games before he hit two against Wigan at Anfield on 3 December.

Crouch was on Spurs' books as a youngster, but it was QPR who gave him his first-team break. His performances for Portsmouth in the old Division One persuaded Aston Villa to give him the chance to show what he could do in the Premiership. Crouch netted only six times in over 40 appearances and Villa sold him for just £2 million – representing a £3 million loss – to Saints in 2004. Since then, his star has been on the rise.

Crouch was called up to the international squad for last summer's American tour, making his debut in the 3–2 win over Colombia. It was Owen's hat-trick which took the headlines, but one of those came from a Crouch assist, and the debutant's overall contribution was impressive.

Rooney and Owen look the likely first-choice pairing, with 6ft 7in Crouch used to unnerve defenders if Plan A isn't working. He is an obvious aerial threat, but his deftness of touch is probably his main asset. He holds the ball up superbly and lays it off with great accuracy, as well as being a goal threat in his own right.

CLUB/POSITION: LIVERPOOL/STRIKER
D.O.B: 30 JAN 1981, MACCLESFIELD
DEBUT: v COLOMBIA, 31 MAY 2005
CAPS/GOALS: 5/1

England's young flyer

A year ago, Shaun Wright-Phillips was on top of the footballing world. He was the biggest fish in the Manchester City pool, and had burst onto the England scene with a brilliant solo goal in the 3–0 victory win over Ukraine at St James' Park the previous August. His exuberant, direct play was breathtakingly refreshing; England at last had a classy, classical winger who could breeze past players at pace and get behind opposition defences. That was something David Beckham didn't have in his locker, and some even felt he ought to unseat the captain in the national side.

Since his £21 million move to Stamford Bridge last summer, things haven't gone quite so well. Wright-Phillips has experienced at first hand Chelsea's ability to park big-name buys on the bench. In the first half of the season he got precious little time on the pitch and was deployed mainly in a substitute role.

At 15 Wright-Phillips was released by Nottingham Forest for being too small, a 'criticism' that was levelled at the young Kevin Keegan, whom he would play under at Manchester City. City were only too keen to take him on, and in his six years at the club he emerged as one of the brightest new talents in the country.

Despite his lack of game time, Sven has kept faith with the young flyer, though the pattern of his international career to date has mirrored his Chelsea experience; he has been used as an impact player rather than a 90-minute man. The prospect of him coming off the bench and taking on tiring defenders is one that could pay big dividends in Germany this summer.

CLUB/POSITION:	CHELSEA/MIDFIELDER
D.O.B:	25 OCTOBER 1981 LONDON
DEBUT:	v UKRAINE, 18 AUGUST 2004
CAPS/GOALS:	8/1

MICHAEL OWEN ENGLAND

Fourth on England's all-time list

Michael Owen's brace in the 3–2 win over Argentina last November took him to 35 in an England shirt, in his 75th appearance. Only Jimmy Greaves, Gary Lineker and Sir Bobby Charlton stand ahead of him in the all-time list. Still only 26, Owen will surely get the 15 goals required to eclipse Charlton's long-standing record before his international career comes to an end, and if he does so, the mantle will have passed to another player who is a fine ambassador for the sport, as well as an ace goal poacher.

Owen was a prodigiously gifted youngster, his 97-goal haul for Deeside Primary School U-11s breaking the record set by another Anfield legend, Ian Rush. Owen signed pro forms for the Reds on his 17th birthday, and scored on his debut, against Wimbledon in May 1997. Twelve months later he was the Premiership's joint-top scorer and a key member of the international side.

Owen made his England debut against Chile on 11 February 1998, aged 18 years and 59 days. The youngest player to be capped in a century soon became the youngest goalscorer, his strike against Morocco in a World Cup warm-up in May increasing the clamour for his inclusion in the starting line-up in France. Coach Glenn Hoddle famously said Owen was 'not a natural goalscorer', but no doubt the latter's breathtaking solo goal against Argentina in the second round went a long way to changing his mind.

The goals and the plaudits kept coming. Who can forget his hat-trick in the stunning 5–1 win in Germany in September 2001? Or the double in that year's FA Cup final against Arsenal, which turned the game on its head.

Such performances helped him win the European Footballer of the Year award, the first Englishman to be thus honoured since Kevin Keegan in 1979.

In his season at the Bernabeu, 2004–05, Owen proved that he was as deadly as any of the big-name Galacticos. He wasn't a regular starter, yet his 13 La Liga goals outshone the likes of Raul and Ronaldo, when the number of minutes on the pitch was taken into account.

Last summer he returned to the Premiership with Newcastle United for a club record £16 million, and soon opened his Magpies account. His season has been blighted by injury, though that could be a boost for England as he should be fresh and full of running when the action gets underway against Paraguay.

CLUB/POSITION:	NEWCASTLE UNITED/STRIKER
D.O.B:	14 DECEMBER 1979, CHESTER
DEBUT:	v CHILE, 11 FEBRUARY 1998
CAPS/GOALS:	75/35

STEVEN GERRARD ENGLAND

World-class attacking midfielder

The fact that Steven Gerrard missed out on Japan and Korea must have been a huge personal disappointment for a player who exhibits such pride and passion when turning out for club and country. It was also a major blow to England's cause, 'Stevie G' being one of the few world-class players in Eriksson's squad.

Four years on, he has, if anything, enhanced his glittering reputation as one of best box-to-box players in the game. Before Rafa Benitez moulded the Reds into a formidable unit once again, there were spells when the team struggled, spells during which Gerrard at times seemed to be playing the opposition on his own.

Last summer, the hot transfer speculation was whether he would sever his ties with his beloved Liverpool in search of club honours. Had he not lifted the Champions League trophy, perhaps his rumoured move to Stamford Bridge might have been realised. But the dramatic, rollercoaster ride of Istanbul brought about a change of heart. Gerrard had been at his inspirational best, scoring one and earning the penalty which Xabi Alonso converted to complete a remarkable comeback. 'How can I leave after that?' was his reaction, affirming his commitment to the club and allowing Reds fans to issue forth a collective sigh of relief.

Gerrard has been at Anfield since he was eight. He made his debut in 1998, though his early career was hampered through injuries that were put down to growth spurts. Even so, it was soon clear that Liverpool had a gem on their hands. England coach Kevin Keegan enthused about Gerrard's performances, and awarded him his first cap in a 2–0 home victory over Ukraine in May 2000. A
year later, under Sven-Goran Eriksson, he fired in a trademark 25-yarder in the memorable 5–1 win in Germany, his first goal in an England shirt.

That a fit Steven Gerrard is an automatic starter for England is a given; where to play him is something that must be exercising the coach's mind. His natural home is driving forward from midfield, either through the centre or on the right flank. The presence of Lampard and Beckham leaves Sven trying to fit a quart into a pint pot, though no doubt a problem that any international manager would willingly embrace.

CLUB/POSITION:	LIVERPOOL/MIDFIELDER
D.O.B:	30 MAY 1980, LIVERPOOL
DEBUT:	v UKRAINE, 31 MAY 2000
CAPS/GOALS:	40/6

MICHAEL CARRICK ENGLAND

Combative tackler with great vision

Going into World Cup year, Michael Carrick had just four caps to his name, two substitute appearances in 2001, and starts against Colombia and USA in the 2005 summer tour of America. However, the fact that Sven seems to be considering playing a holding midfield player may just propel the Spurs man into contention.

Carrick joined the West Ham academy after leaving school, and was a member of the team which won The FA Youth Cup in 1999. He made his senior debut that year, and in 2001–02 he helped the team to seventh place in the Premiership. Along with star team-mates Jermain Defoe and Joe Cole, Carrick became a transfer target after the Hammers were relegated a year later. He gave West Ham another full season before following in Defoe and Freddie Kanoute's footsteps by moving to White Hart Lane.

In his first season at Spurs, Lilywhites fans were treated to the full Carrick repertoire: great vision, accurate distribution, combative tackling. His outstanding form that term earned him starts in the American tour, four years after he had last donned an England shirt.

Eriksson has experimented with another Spurs man, Ledley King, as a holding midfield player, and Beckham has also been tried in a deep-lying position. Carrick has all the attributes required for that anchor role, and a compelling case could be made in his favour. Unlike King, he plays in midfield regularly for his club, and he is a better ball-winner than the skipper, who in any case will be better deployed whipping in vicious crosses from the right flank for the strikers to feed off. Should Sven decide to go for the 'quarter-back' option, the classy Carrick might be a surprise starter instead of second-string squad member.

CLUB/POSITION:	TOTTENHAM H./MIDFIELDER
D.O.B:	28 JULY 1981, WALLSEND
DEBUT:	v MEXICO, 25 MAY 2001
CAPS/GOALS:	5/0

Fit and quick all-rounder

Didier Deschamps, France's World Cup-winning captain in 1998, was famously described by the mercurial Eric Cantona as a 'water carrier'. Brazil's Dunga, who lifted the trophy in 1994, was in the same mould. The midfield needs a balance, creativity and flair tempered with players who cover the ground, put in the tackles and link the play. Owen Hargreaves falls into that category. Eriksson is a long-standing admirer, regularly including Hargreaves in the senior squad during his tenure as England coach.

Hargreaves swapped Calgary Foothills for Bayern Munich at the age of 16. It took him four years to make his breakthrough, and when it finally came, he was given the task of filling the boots of the suspended Stefan Effenberg in the 2001 UEFA Champions League campaign. Effenberg was the heartbeat of the side, and Hargreaves became an instant hero with the fans as he proved to be an able deputy in Bayern's victorious campaign. He has been a first team regular ever since, picking up his third Bundesliga winners' medal in 2005. That year he committed himself to the club until 2010, scotching rumours of a move to the Premiership.

With an English father and Welsh mother, Hargeaves had a big decision to make when it came to the international arena. He could even have turned out for Germany by dint of the residence rule. But he opted for England, making his debut at White Hart Lane in August 2001, in a 2–0 defeat by Holland.

Hargreaves has vital tournament experience, having featured in five of England's games at the 2002 World Cup and Euro 2004. He is one of the fittest and quickest squad members, and with his ability to operate at full back as well as midfield, it is easy to see why Sven rates him so highly.

CLUB/POSITION:	BAYERN MUNICH/MIDFIELDER
D.O.B:	20 JAN 1981, CALGARY, CANADA
DEBUT:	v HOLLAND, 15 AUGUST 2001
CAPS/GOALS:	29/0

JOE COLE ENGLAND

Chelsea regular and virtuoso

Since the last World Cup, no issue has provoked further debate than that of who should occupy the vital role on the left side of England's midfield. Over the past year Joe Cole's form for both club and country has made him favourite for that key piece in Sven's jigsaw. Having made only a cameo 16-minute appearance in Japan and Korea – as substitute in the 1–1 draw with Sweden – and warmed the bench for the entire Euro 2004 jamboree, Cole will be desperate to consolidate his place in Sven's starting line-up in Germany.

Cole was regarded as the pick of a precociously talented crop of young players on West Ham's books in the late 1990s, a group nurtured by Harry Redknapp. He was a member of the Hammers team which won The FA Youth Cup in 1998–99, making his debut for the senior side that same year. His extravagant skills brought deserved praise, though the inevitable 'wonderkid' tag became something of a burden as the team slipped down the Premiership table. Much was heaped on Cole's young shoulders as the Hammers became involved in a relegation dogfight, one they lost in 2002–03.

Cole joined Chelsea in a £6.6 million deal that summer. In his first season at the Bridge he struggled to come to terms with being just another member of an all-star squad, no longer the revered top dog. When Claudio Ranieri 'tinkered', Cole was a casualty too often for his liking, and there were reports that he wanted away from the club. But he has flourished under the tutelage of Jose Mourinho, featuring in 46 games and hitting nine goals in Chelsea's remarkable 2004–05 campaign, which yielded the Carling Cup and Premiership crown.

Eriksson is a self-confessed Cole fan, though his international record shows that he has largely been used as an impact player. In winning his first 20 caps Cole played the full 90 minutes on only three occasions. He is a game-breaker, a player who can slice open a defence with a virtuoso piece of skill or perceptive pass. The flip side is that his lapses are more noticeable than those who choose the safe option. Both aspects were in evidence in the 3–2 home defeat against Denmark in November 2003: Cole scored a terrific goal – his second in an England shirt – but the team also conceded when he lost possession. In the last two years Cole has become a much more consistent performer, at both Premiership and international level, and his flair may well be the key to unlocking the niggardly defences England will face in Germany.

CLUB/POSITION:	**CHELSEA/MIDFIELDER**
D.O.B:	**8 NOVEMBER 1981, ISLINGTON**
DEBUT:	**v MEXICO, 25 MAY 2001**
CAPS/GOALS:	**30/5**

Goal-scoring debut

Jermain Defoe was, arguably, Spurs' player of the season in 2004–05, his first full campaign with the north London club following his £7 million move from West Ham in January 2004. He hit a phenomenal 22 goals in 35 league and cup games, and there were trademark spectacular strikes along with the predatory tap-ins. This term has proved more of a struggle, Defoe suffering as Martin Jol shuffled an attack which included Robbie Keane and Mido. Even so, there have been numerous instances of the pace, trickery and finishing power which will keep Rooney and Owen on their toes.

Defoe was on Charlton's books as a youngster, joining West Ham in 1999 before making a first-team appearance for Alan Curbishley's side. In 2000–01 he had a loan spell with Bournemouth, where he scored in a record ten consecutive league matches. Back at Upton Park he was soon pressing the club's senior strikers Paolo di Canio and Freddie Kanoute for a starting place. Some blistering performances for the England U-21 side helped him stake his claim.

Even Defoe's goals couldn't save the Hammers from relegation in 2003, and he came in for criticism from the fans for immediately slapping in a transfer request. But like Joe Cole, he had given his all for the club, and a sizeable fee allowed West Ham to plan their return to the top flight.

Defoe scored on his first start for England, in the crunch 2–1 away win over Poland in September 2004. That maintained his fine record of getting on the scoresheet in every debut appearance since he joined the professional ranks.

Defoe's stop-start season may have affected his rhythm and confidence. On the other hand, he will be fresh and ready for the challenge if he gets the call to arms from Sven this summer.

CLUB/POSITION: TOTTENHAM HOTSPUR/STRIKER
D.O.B: 7 OCT 1982, BECKTON, LONDON
DEBUT: v SWEDEN, 31 MARCH 2004
CAPS/GOALS: 16/1

FRANK LAMPARD ENGLAND

Player of the Year, 2005

A year into Frank Lampard's Chelsea career, following his move from West Ham in June 2001, the £11 million fee was looking somewhat steep. One of the bright young stars at the Hammers, where his father was assistant manager, the midfielder struggled to impose himself when he first moved to Stamford Bridge. Three years on the price tag looks an absolute steal. 'Super Frankie' has blossomed into one of the most influential players in world football. His place among the elite was recognised at the end of another outstanding year when he was named runner-up to Ronaldinho in the 2005 European Footballer of the Year honours, and short-listed, along with the Brazilian maestro and his Barcelona team-mate Samuel Eto'o, for FIFA's world award.

The fact that Lampard plays in the engine room at a Chelsea side battling on three fronts, and for a manager with a star-studded squad at his disposal, makes Lampard's achievements all the more extraordinary. Jose Mourinho values performance over reputation, and a host of big names have fallen victim to his rotation decisions. But Lampard, like the Bank of England, is always there; solid, reliable, gloriously consistent. Last November he broke David James's Premiership record of 159 consecutive games, marking his 160th with a goal against Portsmouth. Chelsea fans had to go back to September 2001 to find a Lamps-free team sheet. After the game Mourinho said he wouldn't swap his dynamo and playmaker for anyone in the world.

Lampard's guile, superb range of passing and tireless running – not to mention his goals – have been equally to the fore on the international scene. As with his league form, progress was steady. After making his debut against Belgium in 1999, Lampard made just six appearances in the next three years, missing out on both Euro 2000 and the World Cup in Japan and Korea. But since 2003 he has been pivotal in England's two major campaigns. His three goals and excellent performances at Euro 2004 earned him a place in the tournament's all-star squad, and at the end of that season the fans voted him their player of the year.

Lampard's superb volley clinched a 2–1 victory over Poland in the final World Cup qualifier, a result which ensured England topped their group. That strike took Frank into double figures for his country, in his 37th outing. Considering he didn't open his international account until his 12th appearance – against Croatia in August 2003 – Lampard's goals in the last three years have come at a rate which wouldn't disgrace a striker.

After yet another excellent 12 months for both club and country, Lampard was named England's Player of the Year for 2005.

CLUB/POSITION:	CHELSEA/MIDFIELDER
D.O.B:	20 JUNE 1978, ROMFORD
DEBUT:	v BELGIUM, 10 OCTOBER 1999
CAPS/GOALS:	38/10

JERMAINE JENAS ENGLAND

Newcomer makes an impact

Jermaine Jenas was one of a rookie trio who took the field at Upton Park in England's 3–1 defeat by Australia in February 2003. It was his assist which produced England's only bright note in a dismal performance, Francis Jeffers – another of the newcomers – getting on the end of his cross. Jenas had only played 45 minutes, yet his assured display made him the home side's man-of-the-match. Since then, he hasn't quite equalled the spectacular rise of the third new boy that day, Wayne Rooney, but he has established himself as one of the best young midfielders in the land.

Jenas was a product of Nottingham Forest's youth system, making his first-team debut in January 2001, a month short of his 18th birthday. After barely a year in the limelight, in which he earned rave reviews, Jenas was put up for sale by cash-strapped Forest.

Newcastle United boss Bobby Robson had little hesitation in stumping up £5 million for the England U-19 skipper. The 2002–03 season saw Jenas establish himself in the Newcastle team, and he built on the impact made on his England debut by playing a part in England's early-summer victories over South Africa and Serbia and Montenegro.

JJ made three further international appearances during the 2003–04 campaign, but missed out on a place in the Euro 2004 squad. Two years on, he looks a much stronger contender, having enhanced his reputation since his £7 million move to White Hart Lane last August. However, with Beckham, Lampard and Gerrard as fixtures in the engine room, Jenas may be consigned to a bit-part role this summer; indeed, most of his caps have come via the substitutes' bench. Game-breakers who can come on when the opposition is tiring are vital to an international coach's armoury, and Jenas could well be deployed in that role.

CLUB/POSITION:	TOTTENHAM H./MIDFIELDER
D.O.B:	18 FEB 1983, NOTTINGHAM
DEBUT:	v AUSTRALIA, 12 FEB 2003
CAPS/GOALS:	15/0

ENGLAND **LEDLEY KING**

England's versatile defender

Ledley King's performances against Poland in the crunch World Cup qualifier and in the friendly victory over Argentina last autumn have given Sven-Goran Eriksson much food for thought. Beckham, Gerrard, Lampard and Cole had looked to be the first-choice midfield unit, but none of that quartet can play the holding role as well as the Tottenham man. His speed, tackling ability and reading of the game make him a natural defender, and the extra protection he offers the back four may just persuade Sven to sacrifice one of his more attacking players, or to make a switch if England take the lead and need to consolidate. Beckham and Gerrard were missing for the 2–1 win over Poland, while King played for the first hour against Argentina before being replaced by Cole. Having them all fit will be a welcome problem for the England coach.

King made his Spurs debut as an 18-year-old, and became a first-team regular in 2000–01. His manager, ex-England coach Glenn Hoddle, was soon tipping him as a future international, and it didn't take long for that prediction to come true. King got his first start in the 2–1 home defeat by Italy in March 2002. His second outing saw another reverse on home soil, against Australia in February 2003. A year later he marked his first full appearance by scoring England's goal in the 1–1 draw in Portugal.

King was outstanding against France in England's opening Euro 2004 match, despite the fact that the 1998 world champions snatched a late victory. That day he was in central defence, where he plays most of his club football. In a 23-man World Cup squad versatility is a prized asset, and even if he doesn't make the starting line-up, King's multi-faceted game will boost England's chances in Germany.

CLUB/POSITION:	TOTTENHAM H./DEFENDER MIDFIELDER
D.O.B:	12 OCTOBER 1980, BOW, LONDON
DEBUT:	v ITALY, 27 MARCH 2002
CAPS/GOALS:	16/1

JOHN TERRY ENGLAND

Chelsea's inspirational captain

It is a testament to the outstanding form John Terry has shown in the last three years that the pecking order for centre-back in the England side has undergone a radical transformation. Where once the Campbell-Ferdinand axis seemed unbreakable, now those two, plus the other contenders in a position where England have an embarrassment of riches, seem to be vying for a place alongside Chelsea's inspirational captain.

'JT' forced his way into the international reckoning after producing consistently polished displays at the heart of the Blues' cosmopolitan defence. A Chelsea trainee, Terry was originally a midfielder, but as he matured found he had the physique, temperament and qualities required of a top central defender. He first filled that position as a stand-in for the youth team, and it quickly became his natural home. He made his senior debut under Gianluca Vialli, though it was during the Claudio Ranieri era that he became a regular in the side. That was no mean achievement, Chelsea boasting the talents of World Cup-winning stars Marcel Desailly and Frank Leboeuf at the time.

If Ranieri rated his young lion-hearted defender, Jose Mourinho went even further when he took over at Stamford Bridge in the summer of 2004. Mourinho handed Terry the captain's armband, and during Chelsea's record-breaking campaign acclaimed him as the best centre-back in world football. The PFA certainly agreed that he was the pick of the bunch domestically, making him the first defender in 12 years to receive the Player of the Year award.

Terry led from the front as Chelsea romped to their first championship in 50 years, scoring a number of crucial goals in his forays upfield as well as being a rock in the heart of the defence.

He missed out on a place in the squad for Japan and Korea, pulling on an England shirt for the first time as substitute against Serbia and Montenegro in June 2003. He made his first full appearance in the home victory over Croatia two months later. At Euro 2004 Ferdinand's absence through suspension left Terry to form a formidable partnership with Sol Campbell at the back. Despite not being fully fit, he put in three typically sure-footed displays.

England's chances in Germany will hinge on the defence's ability to shackle the world's most feared strikers; before the tournament is over some of those will learn what it feels like to have JT breathing down their necks.

CLUB/POSITION:	CHELSEA/DEFENDER
D.O.B:	7 DECEMBER 1980, BARKING
DEBUT:	v SERBIA AND MONTENEGRO, 3 JUNE 2003
CAPS/GOALS:	22/0

RIO FERDINAND ENGLAND

'Rolls-Royce' Rio

Described by former manager Harry Redknapp as a 'Rolls-Royce' of a defender, Rio Ferdinand has attracted the kind of premium associated with that quality marque. His moves from West Ham to Leeds in 2000, and to Old Trafford two years later, cost the purchasing clubs almost £50 million in total, both transfers setting a new British record. Rio has lived up to his expensive billing, his performances displaying the kind of elegance and dependability reminiscent of Upton Park legend Bobby Moore.

Ferdinand was a graduate of the famous Hammers academy, making his debut as a 17-year-old in May 1996. Within eighteen months he had been called up to the England squad, earning his first cap as a substitute in a friendly against Cameroon in November 1997. His silky skills on the ball made him a natural in the international arena, and he has grown in stature over the past nine years.

Rio played in all five games in Japan and Korea, his commanding partnership with Sol Campbell anchoring England's run to the last eight. He put the icing on the cake with his first international goal, in the 3–0 win over Denmark in the second round.

Ferdinand picked up a Premier League championship medal in his first season at Old Trafford, 2002–03. Failure to attend a routine drugs test in September 2003 cost him eight months out of the game, a period which included Euro 2004. Campbell and Terry provided England with a solid platform in his absence, though a fit and in-form Ferdinand is a certain starter. Some pundits have pondered on the merit of playing three centre-backs in a 3–5–2 formation, though Eriksson appears set against that option. A stronger possibility is to deploy Ferdinand as the holding midfield player, a position he has occasionally occupied for United this season.

CLUB/POSITION:	MANCHESTER UNITED/DEFENDER
D.O.B:	7 NOVEMBER 1978, PECKHAM
DEBUT:	v CAMEROON, 15 NOVEMBER 1997
CAPS/GOALS:	45/1

ENGLAND **GARY NEVILLE**

Acclaimed defender set for top 10

The strong partnership between Gary Neville and David Beckham on the right flank was for many years a pillar of the all-conquering Manchester United side, and their excellent understanding remains a strength of the international side.

Few players can match the honours Neville has accumulated since he made his United debut against Torpedo Moscow in a UEFA Cup tie in 1992. It began with victory in the Youth Cup that year, as a member of the side which produced a galaxy of future stars. Since then, there have been eight Premiership titles, four FA Cup winners' medals, and, of course, the celebrated Champions League success of 1999. Neville was first capped in the Venables era in the run-up to Euro '96, and successive England coaches have recognised the quality he brings to the defence; the World Cup should see him top the 80-cap mark, putting him in the all-time top 10 for England appearances. He has already added one more honour this term, taking over as club captain when Roy Keane left Old Trafford last autumn.

Neville has featured in four major tournaments for England: Euro 96, the 1998 World Cup, Euro 2000 and Euro 2004; injury forced him to miss Japan and Korea 2002. Apart from his wealth of international experience, Neville has also clocked up over a hundred games in European club competition, pitting his wits against many of the strikers who will grace the World Cup finals. He has also proved on many occasions that he is an accomplished central defender, and although England hardly have a dearth of talent in that area, it does expand Sven's options when players can operate in more than one position.

Wherever he plays, Neville will be an invaluable asset, both for his personal contribution and as a mentor to the younger squad members.

CLUB/POSITION:	MANCHESTER UNITED/DEFENDER
D.O.B;	18 FEBRUARY 1975, BURY
DEBUT:	v JAPAN, 3 JUNE 1995
CAPS/GOALS:	78/0

ASHLEY COLE ENGLAND

England's world-class defender

If the left side of midfield has exercised the mind of the England coach in recent years, left back has been much less problematic. Since making his international debut as a 20-year-old, Ashley Cole has developed into a cultured defender whose surging runs also add a vital dimension to England's offensive play. Cole is seen as the natural successor to the two best attacking left backs in the world over the past 15 years, AC Milan's Paolo Maldini and Roberto Carlos of Real Madrid. Those in charge at the Bernabeu are known admirers of the Arsenal man, and are keeping a watchful eye on a player they see as a potential replacement for the veteran Brazilian.

Should Cole decide to leave Highbury, Real may face competition from Roman Abramovich's deep pockets. Last year Cole was fined by the Premier League for an unauthorised meeting with Chelsea officials, but he remained as committed as ever to the Gunners' cause, even signing an extension to his contract in August 2005. That unsettled period is now behind him, which can only augur well for Sven and England this summer.

Cole joined Arsenal as a teenager, making his debut for the first team as an 18-year-old early in the 1999–2000 campaign. He had a loan spell at Crystal Palace that season, but by 2000 he had replaced Silvinho as the club's first-choice left-back. He already has two Premiership and three FA Cup winners' medals under his belt.

Cole has been an England regular under Sven, and featured in every game at the 2002 World Cup and Euro 2004. In the latter tournament his performances earned him a place in UEFA's all-star line-up, one of four England players to be thus honoured.

CLUB/POSITION:	ARSENAL/DEFENDER
D.O.B:	20 DEC 1980, STEPNEY
DEBUT:	v ALBANIA, 28 MARCH 2001
CAPS/GOALS:	44/0

JAMIE CARRAGHER ENGLAND

Fierce competitor ready to challenge

Steven Gerrard's swash-buckling performances in Liverpool's midfield in recent years have attracted rave reviews and filled acres of newsprint; but Reds fans and football insiders rate Jamie Carragher's contribution to Liverpool's resurgence just as highly. In fact, many made Carragher their player of the season in Liverpool's glory year, which culminated in the Champions League triumph in Istanbul in 2005.

An Anfield trainee, Carragher made his Premiership debut in the 1996–97 season and has since clocked up over 400 appearances for Liverpool. Centre-back is obviously his preferred position, but as Sven has an embarrassment of riches in the heart of the defence, Carragher may well be pressed into service at full-back or even as a midfield anchor, where he has shown he can be an equally effective and consistent performer.

Carragher won a record 27 caps for the England U-21 team, and had just turned that age when he won his first senior cap, in a 1–1 draw in Hungary in April 1999. He missed out on Euro 2000, and though he was a regular squad member in the qualifiers for the 2002 World Cup, injury put paid to his chance of going to Japan and Korea. He recovered from a broken leg early in the 2003–04 season to force his way into the squad for the European Championship, but didn't see any action in Portugal.

Carragher already has a sizeable medal collection, having won both domestic cup competitions, the UEFA Cup, European Super Cup, and, of course, the Champions League. At club level the Premiership title is the obvious target; on the international front this committed, fierce competitor will strain every sinew for the World Cup cause, and having shown his mettle against Europe's top strikers, he undoubtedly has quality commensurate with his drive and passion.

CLUB/POSITION: LIVERPOOL/DEFENDER
D.O.B.: 28 JAN 1978, BOOTLE, LIVERPOOL
DEBUT: v HUNGARY, 28 APRIL 1999
CAPS/GOALS: 23/0

ENGLAND   SOL CAMPBELL

England's big-match defender

The old adage 'form is temporary, class is permanent' could undoubtedly be given an airing to describe Sol Campbell's season. He suffered a dip in confidence and drop in performance level, culminating in the 3–2 home defeat by West Ham in February. Campbell was at fault for the first two goals and substituted at half-time, leaving Highbury without even waiting for the final whistle.

A temporary blip shouldn't detract from the enormous contribution Sol has made to the England cause in the past decade. He has been a towering presence in the heart of the defence, and in the major tournaments he has been one of England's key performers. He made a cameo appearance in Terry Venables' Euro '96 squad, but it was at France '98 that he truly made his mark. He almost capped a sure-footed defensive display with a winner against Argentina, but his header was ruled out for an infringement by Shearer.

In 2001 Campbell showed his mettle by leaving White Hart Lane, the club he had been with since boyhood, in search of honours with arch-rivals Arsenal. His decision was vindicated as he helped the Gunners to the double in his debut season.

Campbell finally opened his England account in the 1–1 draw with Sweden at the 2002 World Cup. In the Euro 2004 quarter-final against hosts Portugal he had a late header chalked off when the score was 1–1. The game was lost, but Campbell was named in UEFA's All-Star XI.

Germany will see Campbell make a record sixth appearance in a major tournament. The Terry-Ferdinand partnership, which blossomed during Campbell's injury-hit 2005, means he is no longer an automatic choice, but he is a big-match player and will no doubt make a vital contribution to the World Cup cause.

CLUB/POSITION:	ARSENAL/DEFENDER
D.O.B:	18 SEPTEMBER 1974, NEWHAM
DEBUT:	v HUNGARY, 18 MAY 1996
CAPS/GOALS:	66/1

PAUL ROBINSON ENGLAND

Brave and agile number one

Paul Robinson's outstanding form for Spurs over the past two years has made him England's first-choice goalkeeper. Robinson has all the hallmarks of a top 'keeper: great agility, sharp reflexes, good positional sense and unflinching bravery. And, crucially, a very low error count.

Robinson started his career at Leeds United, for whom he made his debut in 1998. During the turbulent period at Elland Road in which David O'Leary's all-star side was dismantled to balance the books, Robinson maintained his excellent form. He was, naturally, one of the prize assets, and Leeds finally cashed in following relegation in May 2004, Tottenham picking up a £1.5 million bargain.

By then, Robinson was already an international, having made his debut as a second-half substitute for David James in the 3–1 defeat against Australia at Upton Park in February 2003. After three more substitute appearances over the next 12 months, Robinson made his full debut in a 6–1 home victory over Iceland in June 2004. He was part of the Euro 2004 squad, though as second-string to James, who was still England's number one. Those positions were reversed in 2005, and 26-year-old Robinson goes to Germany as the undisputed man in possession.

England's World Cup history is littered with key moments involving goalkeepers: Peter Bonetti might have done better in the 3–2 quarter-final defeat by West Germany in 1970; Peter Shilton was beaten by Poland's Domarski in the famous 1973 qualifier, and outjumped by Maradona in the 'hand of God' incident at Mexico '86; and four years ago, Ronaldinho's free kick floated over David Seaman's head to put Brazil into the semis. Goalkeepers can win and lose matches, and England are fortunate to have such a talented and consistent performer between the sticks.

CLUB/POSITION:	TOTTENHAM H./GOALKEEPER
D.O.B.:	15 OCT 1979, BEVERLEY, YORKSHIRE
DEBUT:	v AUSTRALIA, 12 FEBRUARY 2003
CAPS/GOALS:	19/0

Premiership record breaker

The moniker 'Calamity James' will undoubtedly attend the Manchester City 'keeper for the rest of his career, though he is, for the main part, simply a victim of his position: goalkeepers take the flak, while errors made by outfield players dwindle much more readily. James has played in the top flight since the Premiership was formed, with the exception of a brief spell following West Ham's relegation in 2003. During his time with Liverpool, he set a Premiership record by making 159 consecutive appearances, a mark eclipsed only this season by Frank Lampard.

The man rated by Manchester City manager Stuart Pearce as one of the top three 'keepers in England made his breakthrough thanks to a much earlier transfer to Maine Road. It was when Tony Coton joined City that James got his chance at Watford. A £1 million move to Liverpool came in 1992, and though his seven years at Anfield produced the odd high-profile howler, James did enough to warrant an international call-up. That was in March 1997, a 2–0 home win over against Mexico.

For the next five years James remained the understudy to David Seaman, and it was only after the latter's retirement following the 2002 World Cup that he finally made the England jersey his own. Ironically, Seaman's retirement while playing for Manchester City also paved the way for James' return to Premiership action, as he joined the club from West Ham in January 2004.

James was ever-present in England's run to the quarters at Euro 2004, but lost his place to Paul Robinson after the disastrous 4–1 defeat by Denmark last August. He remains bullish about his chances of regaining the No.1 spot, determined to maintain his excellent form for City and give Eriksson a poser when it comes to picking the team to face Paraguay on 10 June.

CLUB/POSITION:	MANCHESTER CITY/GOALKEEPER
D.O.B.:	1 AUGUST 1970, WELWYN
DEBUT:	v MEXICO, 29 MARCH 1997
CAPS/GOALS:	33/0

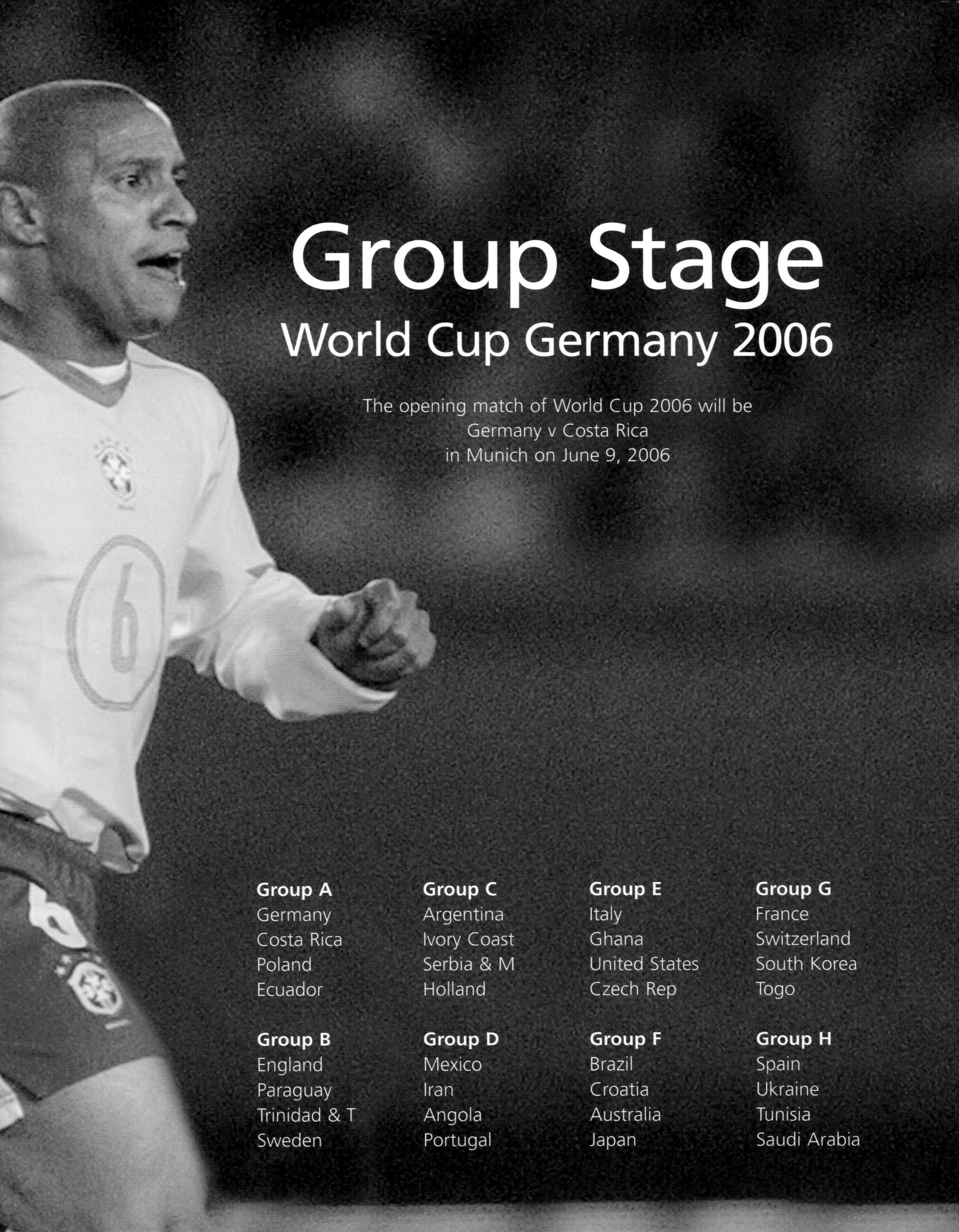

Group Stage
World Cup Germany 2006

The opening match of World Cup 2006 will be
Germany v Costa Rica
in Munich on June 9, 2006

Group A
Germany
Costa Rica
Poland
Ecuador

Group B
England
Paraguay
Trinidad & T
Sweden

Group C
Argentina
Ivory Coast
Serbia & M
Holland

Group D
Mexico
Iran
Angola
Portugal

Group E
Italy
Ghana
United States
Czech Rep

Group F
Brazil
Croatia
Australia
Japan

Group G
France
Switzerland
South Korea
Togo

Group H
Spain
Ukraine
Tunisia
Saudi Arabia

Group A

Germany

Poland

Costa Rica

Ecuador

Friday June 9 Munich and Gelsenkirchen
Germany v Costa Rica, Poland v Ecuador

Wednesday June 14 Dortmund
Germany v Poland

Thursday June 15 Hamburg
Ecuador v Costa Rica

Tuesday June 20 Berlin and Hanover
Ecuador v Germany, Costa Rica v Poland

GERMANY FIFA ranking: 19 • World Cup history: 16th appearance

Klinsmann keen to match 'Kaiser'

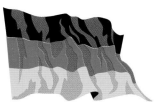

'Never write off Germany' is a footballing maxim which in terms of longevity is right up there with 'a game of two halves' and 'take each game as it comes'. And when the team has the advantage of playing on home territory, that old saying almost becomes an immutable law of physics – September 2001 being a glorious exception.

With no qualifying campaign by which to gauge the current state of the national side, one has to go back to the last World Cup and Euro 2004 for the most recent tournament form guide. That gives a curate's egg of a picture: surprise finalists in Japan and Korea, dumped out of Portugal 2004 at the first hurdle, without a win to their name and held to a goalless draw by the minnows of Latvia.

That poor showing brought a change of coach. Exit Rudi Voller, enter his teammate from the 1990 World Cup-winning side, Jurgen Klinsmann. The former Spurs striker wasn't the number one choice; the German FA turned to him only after veteran coach Ottmar Hitzfeld chose to take a sabbatical and put family before football.

Klinsmann, like Alf Ramsey prior to 1966, is predicting victory for his side, repeating the country's home success of 1974. If he pulls it off he will emulate the achievement of the captain of that great side of 32 years ago, the legendary Franz Beckenbauer. 'Der Kaiser' also took over as coach of the national team with no club experience, and under his guidance Germany did rather well: runners-up to a Maradona-inspired Argentina in 1986, winners four years later in Italy, beating the same opposition in the final.

There are many dissenting voices about the current regime, however. Bayern Munich general manager Uli Hoeness, another stalwart of the 1970s Germany side, expresses the opinion of many when he says that the Klinsmann appointment was born from crisis, and 'the national team is a catastrophe'. The coach hasn't done himself any PR favours by his much-publicised decision to spend three weeks of each month at his California home, when many felt he should have been doing the rounds of the Bundesliga, trawling for talent to galvanise a squad which many feel isn't good enough to go the distance this time. It is doubtful that the harbingers of doom were much placated by Klinsmann's announcement that he wanted the team to wear red shirts instead of the traditional white. Red may well be more associated with a positive attitude and aggression, but a metaphor involving carts and horses – or the Teutonic equivalent – doubtless sprang to the minds of those more concerned with the quality of the players on the pitch.

Above: German players celebrate after Schweinsteiger scores during the Confederations Cup against Mexico.

GERMANY Winners: 1954, 1974, 1990

Six out of the last 10 finals

Last year's Confederations Cup did provide some encouragement, though. Germany's most recent competitive experience – also on home soil – saw the team draw with Argentina at the group stage and only go down to Brazil in the semis by the odd goal in five. Cologne striker Lukas Podolski and Michael Ballack were the men on target against the reigning world champions, and much is expected of them this summer.

As ever, Oliver Kahn and Arsenal's Jens Lehmann will probably dispute the goalkeeping jersey. The defence look far from impenetrable, particularly if Klinsmann opts for Chelsea's cameo-man Robert Huth and Lukas Sinkiewicz of Cologne in the centre. The Bayern Munich trio of Ballack, Sebastian Deisler and Bastian Schweinsteiger, along with Bayer Leverkusen's Bernd Schneider, will run the midfield show; Thomas Hitzlsperger, the former Aston Villa man now with Stuttgart, may also get the opportunity to unleash the shooting power which earned him the nickname 'Der Hammer', though Didi Hamann doesn't seem to figure in Klinsmann's plans. Up front, Klinsmann will look to Podolski and Schalke 04's Kevin Kuranyi, along with Miroslav Klose, the man who came from nowhere to be one of the stars of the 2002 tournament.

Klinsmann can have no complaints about the draw. Even if this is not a vintage German side, it will doubtless prove much too strong for Costa Rica, Poland and Ecuador. A solid start might just give the team the momentum to reach the latter stages, though the country that has contested six of the last 10 finals probably lacks the overall class to add to that remarkable tally.

STAR PLAYER

Sebastian Deisler
D.O.B. 5 January 1980

Even the most partisan supporter of any of Germany's opponents this summer will surely wish Sebastian Deisler well, if not the team as a whole. This gifted midfielder, who was once lauded as highly as his club and international teammate Michael Ballack, has had to contend with career-threatening knee injuries, and chronic depression. The road to recovery began with the birth of his first child, and in the past year he has regained the form which prompted Bayern Munich to chase his signature in 2002, the summer in which Ballack also joined the club.

Deisler joined Borussia Moenchengladbach from his home-town club FV Lorrach in 1995. In the wake of Germany's 3–0 drubbing by Croatia in the quarter-final of the 1998 World Cup, Deisler was seen as one of the great hopes of the next generation. While the senior team was packing its bags in France, Deisler was helping Germany to reach the final of the UEFA U-18 Championship. He was fast-tracked into the full Germany team, winning his first cap barely 18 months later.

Deisler joined Hertha Berlin in 1999 and played in the Germany side which was dumped out of the following year's European Championship as group wooden spoonists. A recurring knee injury cost him a place at the 2002 World Cup finals, and it also limited his appearances for his new club, Bayern, as they completed the domestic double. The unlucky Deisler also missed out on Euro 2004, a season blighted by those psychological as well as physical problems.

He was back in Jurgen Klinsmann's fold for the 2005 Confederations Cup, a season in which Bayern coach Felix Magath had used him sparingly in yet another double-winning campaign. He featured in six international friendlies last autumn, suggesting that at long last Deisler may be about to fulfil the promise which led one of his early coaches to suggest he might one day be mentioned in the same breath as Beckenbauer.

GERMANY

STAR PLAYER
Michael Ballack
D.O.B. 26 September 1976

Michael Ballack will need to lead from the front if Germany is to be in the shake-up when the World Cup reaches the business end. With Oliver Kahn about to turn 37, the captain is the team's one truly world-class player, the man who drove a fairly ordinary Germany side to the semis four years ago. In Japan and Korea he netted the winning goal in both the quarter-final and the semis, against the USA and South Korea respectively. Suspension forced him to miss the final, but his three goals and four assists remained the best return of any midfielder on show.

Born in East Germany, Ballack began his career as a young boy with Chemnitz. Kaiserslautern spotted his potential and gave him his Bundesliga debut, in 1997–98, when the team had just returned to the top flight. Otto Rehhagel's side set a record by winning the championship that season, the first promoted side to do so.

It was during his three years at Bayer Leverkusen, whom he joined in 1999, that Ballack emerged as the hottest property in German football. His final season with the club before joining Bayern Munich in summer 2002 was extraordinary: in addition to the World Cup disappointment, Ballack had a triple helping of agony with his club, who finished second in the league, runners-up in the German cup, and lost to Real Madrid in the Champions League final. Ballack at least had the consolation of winning the first of his three domestic Footballer of the Year awards; only Beckenbauer has bettered that. Ballack has also twice won the double with the Bavarian giants, so his haul of winners medals has improved significantly in the past four years.

He began World Cup year with 29 goals to his name, from just 61 games for his country. He is the linchpin, yet, curiously, there is a school of thought that feels he should have delivered even more. No less a figure than Pele has said he doesn't think Ballack has progressed in recent seasons. Klinsmann fiercely defends his playmaker, whom he predicts will cement his place among the midfield greats this summer.

POLAND   FIFA ranking: 26 • World Cup history: 7th appearance

27-goal haul in qualification

Everybody remembers the fact that Poland came to Wembley in 1973 and escaped with a 1–1 draw, a result that meant England missed out on the 1974 World Cup. Probably more hazy in the recollection is that Lato, Szarmach, Deyna and Co. lit up the tournament, won six of their seven matches – including the scalps of Argentina and Brazil – and only missed out on a place in the final by going down 1–0 to hosts West Germany in the second group phase decider.

Eight years later, in the Boniek era, Poland again lost to the eventual winners in the semis, Italy on that occasion. It means that since 1966, the Poles have a better World Cup record than England, the team they are so often matched with in tournament qualifiers.

It was Poland who made the running this time round, leading Group Six until the very last hurdle. They went to Old Trafford having won eight of their nine matches, the only hiccup coming in the 2–1 home defeat to England a year earlier. The Poles thus did the double over each of the other four sides in the group, something Erikkson's men failed to do. But in the crunch match in Manchester to decide who would top the table, Poland went down 2–1. Tomasz Frankowski's volley cancelled out Michael Owen's opener before Frank Lampard hit a sweet winner. The result was a repeat of the scoreline in Katowice, but the Poles had done enough to secure one of the two best second-place spots up for grabs.

Pawel Janas will be looking for a huge improvement on 2002, when Poland performed badly under the previous coaching regime. By the time they hit their straps with a 3–1 win over USA, they had already lost to South Korea and Portugal and the plane was waiting on the tarmac.

The Polish side is hardly replete with stars. One of the key players will be Frankowski, the fans' favourite whose goals helped Poland to the fourth best total in the Euro zone. A tally of 27 was 10 more than England managed, and only Portugal, Sweden and the Czech Republic found the net more often. The goalkeeper looks likely to be familiar to British fans. Artur Boruc, who joined Celtic from Legia Warsaw, seems to have displaced Jerzy Dudek, with West Brom's Tomasz Kuszczak also in contention. The side is led by experienced defender Tomasz Klos, who has played in the Bundesliga, and for Guy Roux's Auxerre in France's top division.

The Poles will be resilient, and with Ecuador and Costa Rica in the mix in Group A, they will fancy their chances of reaching the second round for the first time since those heady days of Spain '82. On the other hand, should Janas's men achieve that goal, their Group B opponents in the last 16 won't be quaking in their boots – and that, of course, could well be England.

PATH TO THE FINALS:

RUNNER-UP IN EUROPE GROUP 6

	P	W	D	L	F	A	PTS
ENGLAND	10	8	1	1	17	5	25
POLAND	10	8	0	2	27	9	24
AUSTRIA	10	4	3	3	15	12	15
N IRELAND	10	2	3	5	10	18	9
WALES	10	2	2	6	10	15	8
AZERBAIJAN	10	0	3	7	1	21	3

POLAND

STAR PLAYER

Jacek Krzynowek

D.O.B. 15 May 1976

Jacek Krzynowek is a cultured left-sided midfielder whom coach Pawel Janas believes will be one of his key men in Germany. Krzynowek already has three World Cup games under his belt, having played in each of Poland's matches in Japan and Korea. Like all his compatriots, he no doubt will happily forget the 2–0 defeat by South Korea and the 4–0 drubbing at the hands of Portugal. He will have fonder memories of the final encounter, when he was the best player on the pitch as Poland salvaged some pride by beating the USA 3–1.

Krzynowek, who was first capped in 1998, helped get Poland's 2006 campaign off to a flying start with a fine display and a goal in the 3–0 win over Northern Ireland in Belfast – a result Sven would have been only too pleased to replicate last autumn. Janas had special praise for his performance that day, the player having had little pre-match preparation owing to the death of his father.

Krzynowek went into that game, in September 2004, having just helped FC Nuremburg regain their place in the Bundesliga. His superb form in the club's promotion-winning campaign earned him a move to Bayer Leverkusen, and in one of his first outings, just prior to the game in Belfast, he gave a star performance as Leverkusen thrashed mighty Bayern Munich 4–1. Real Madrid will also have cause to remember him, for the rocket he scored against them in a 3–0 win in the 2004–05 Champions League group stage. Leverkusen topped a group that also included Dynamo Kyiv and Roma, before going down to Liverpool in the last 16.

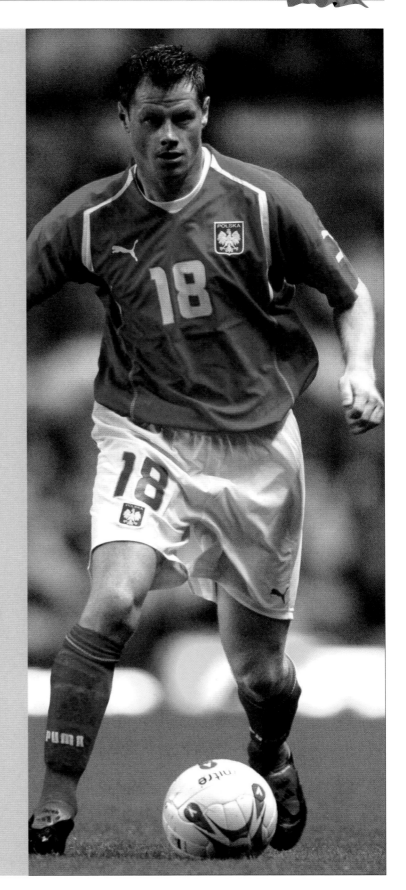

COSTA RICA   FIFA ranking: 25 • World Cup history: 3rd appearance

Third place sees 'Ticos' through

Italia '90 is etched on the memories of Scotland fans as the tournament in which their team was humbled by debutants Costa Rica. Less well remembered is the fact that the 'Ticos' also beat Sweden – something England hasn't managed to do since 1968 – and only lost 1–0 to Brazil.

Costa Rica has been CONCACAF champions ten times, though not since the launch of the Gold Cup in 1991, which made the competition much stiffer. Runner-up to the USA in 2002 is their best showing in the modern era. That year brought a second World Cup adventure, the Ticos unluckily drawn with Brazil and Turkey, who finished winners and third respectively.

The road to Germany began with a nervy away-goals win over Cuba in the preliminary round. The Ticos then came through a group including Guatemala, Honduras and Canada to reach the final six-team eliminator. A last-minute goal by Roy Myre gave the Ticos their only win in the first four matches, at home to Panama, and automatic qualification was in the balance.

Re-enter coach Alexandre Guimaraes, who played in 1990 and led the team to Japan and Korea. His return sparked a run of four wins in five matches, the 3–0 win over the USA in San Jose securing the Ticos' place in the finals.

Playmaker Walter Centeno is a survivor from the last World Cup, along with defender Jervis Drummond and striker Ronald Gomez – the man known as 'The Bullet'. 35-year-old centre-back Ronald Gonzalez also played at Italia '90, where he got on the scoresheet.

Costa Rica will fancy their chances of getting results against Poland and Ecuador and making it through to the knockout stage again, along with Group A favourites Germany.

STAR PLAYER

Paulo Wanchope
D.O.B. 31 July 1976

Currently leading the line for Qatar side Al-Gharafa, Paulo Wanchope remains the biggest name in Costa Rican football. Many fans will remember the gangly 20-year-old who scored against Manchester Utd on his debut for Derby County in 1996–97. Pundits scratched their heads; he could look a world-beater one minute, inept the next.

After three seasons with the Rams, and a brief spell at West Ham, Wanchope moved to Manchester City. He helped City win promotion to the Premiership in 2001–02, then led the Costa Rican attack at Japan and Korea, scoring in the 5–2 defeat by Brazil.

Four years on he is still the premier striker. He top-scored with eight goals in the qualifiers, making a career haul of 43 goals in 66 appearances. Wanchope says Germany will be his international swansong, and if the positive side of the enigma is on view, it just might help the team spring a surprise.

PATH TO THE FINALS:

THIRD IN CONCACAF FINAL QUALIFYING GROUP

	P	W	D	L	F	A	PTS
USA	10	7	1	2	16	6	22
MEXICO	10	7	1	2	22	9	22
COSTA RICA	10	5	1	4	15	14	16
TRINIDAD & TOBAGO	10	4	1	5	10	15	13
GUATEMALA	10	3	2	5	16	18	11
PANAMA	10	0	2	8	4	21	2

ECUADOR   FIFA ranking: 38 • World Cup history: 2nd appearance

The altitude kings

Ecuador propped up its group on its World Cup debut four years ago, but the country did score a fine win over Croatia, and finished only a point behind Italy.

Once again, qualification was founded on results at fortress Quito, whose rarefied atmosphere proved too much for a host of big-name visitors. Both Brazil and Argentina left empty handed, Ecuador taking 23 points from 27 at home. The team's only win on its travels also came at altitude, against a struggling Bolivia. Qualification was secured with a game to spare, and a draw in Chile in the final round saw Ecuador swap places with Paraguay to finish an impressive third behind Brazil and Argentina.

Top performers include centre-back Giovany Espinoza, the only South American player to feature in all 18 matches. Alongside him is skipper Ivan Hurtado, a cultured defender with well over 100 caps to his name. National hero Agustin Delgado may be past his best, though the Southampton man still emerged as Ecuador's joint-top scorer in the qualifiers. Aston Villa's Ulises de La Cruz will also provide valuable experience to the crop of rising stars such as Franklin Salas.

The lowest-ranked of the four South American qualifiers, Ecuador has little experience of playing in Europe. It will be a steep learning curve against the hosts, and Poland and Costa Rica are also ranked much higher. Group A looks unlikely to produce an upset.

STAR PLAYER

Edison Méndez
D.O.B. 16 March 1979

Edison Méndez made history when he slotted home the goal which beat Croatia in Japan and Korea, Ecuador's maiden World Cup victory. Méndez's man-of-the-match performance wasn't enough to prevent an early exit, but victory over the team which finished third at France '98 was a huge psychological boost for a country just emerging on the world stage.

Mendez was on top form during the qualifiers this time round, too. He hit a 35-yard rocket in the 5–2 win over Paraguay, helping Ecuador come back from a 2–0 deficit. He also scored the only goal of the game in the home win over Brazil, and having been a member of the team which qualified ahead of Ronaldo, Ronaldinho and Co. in 2002, his record against the world champions is better than most.

Mendez has admirably filled the void left by 'El Maestro' Alex Aguinaga, who retired from international football following the 2002 World Cup. His silky midfield skills and fierce shooting make him one of the key men in Luis Fernando Suarez's squad.

PATH TO THE FINALS:

THIRD PLACE IN SOUTH AMERICAN GROUP

	P	W	D	L	F	A	PTS
BRAZIL	18	9	7	2	35	17	34
ARGENTINA	18	10	4	4	29	17	34
ECUADOR	18	8	4	6	23	19	28
PARAGUAY	18	8	4	6	23	23	28
URUGUAY	18	6	7	5	23	28	25
COLOMBIA	18	6	6	6	24	16	24
CHILE	18	5	7	6	18	22	22
VENEZUELA	18	5	3	10	20	28	18
PERU	18	4	6	8	20	28	18
BOLIVIA	18	4	2	12	20	37	14

Group B

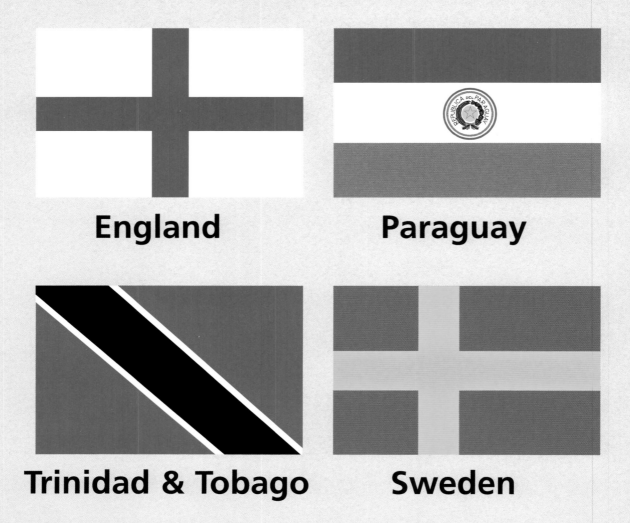

England

Paraguay

Trinidad & Tobago

Sweden

Saturday June 10 Frankfurt and Dortmund
England v Paraguay, Trinidad & Tobago v Sweden

Thursday June 15 Nuremberg and Berlin
England v Trinidad & Tobago, Sweden v Paraguay

Tuesday June 20 Cologne and Kaiserslautern
Sweden v England, Paraguay v Trinidad & Tobago

ENGLAND FIFA ranking: 9 • World Cup history: 12th appearance

Old rivals pose a threat

The draw was kind enough. England may not have beaten Sweden since 1968, but Paraguay and Trinidad and Tobago should hold few terrors. The South American side qualified fourth in the CONMEBOL zone, is the 20th-ranked country of the 32 qualifiers, and has lost both its previous matches against England. For the minnows of Trinidad and Tobago, simply qualifying for Germany was cause for a national holiday; that says much for a tiny country which, if it glances down the rankings, finds only Togo and Angola below it.

There is a school of thought which rather hopes Sweden maintains its record against England, for the Group B runners-up would find themselves in the opposite side of the draw from Brazil, assuming the reigning world champions successfully negotiate a path through Croatia, Australia and Japan. On the other hand, attempting to second-guess quarter- and semi-final encounters heaps if upon if to a mind-boggling extent; if a team aspires to be the best, it has to beat the best.

Four years ago, Sven was denied the services of the multi-talented Steven Gerrard, while David Beckham was carrying an injury. Joe Cole has made the troublesome left side his own with a number of impressive displays. Add in Frank Lampard, runner-up in last autumn's European and World Footballer of the Year awards, and England has a midfield to rival any on show this summer. Accommodating them all might present the coach with a poser. Will Eriksson assign someone to the holding role, possibly bringing Ledley King into the equation? Might the captain be deployed in a quarter-back role, as he was in the 1–0 win against Wales at the Millennium Stadium last September? Or will he ask his star trio to interchange?

Defensively, the team looks strong. A host of talented centre-backs, including Rio Ferdinand, Sol Campbell and Jamie Carragher, will go into the tournament vying for a place alongside John Terry, who looks a certain starter. Sven has scotched the idea of playing three at the back; 4–4–2 is his preferred formation. Ashley Cole, whose season has been blighted by injury, will be raring to go. Gary Neville, another absentee four years ago, adds vast experience to the defence, and his near-telepathic understanding with Beckham from their many years as United team-mates is a plus going forward. Paul Robinson is a worthy addition to the long line of outstanding goalkeepers England has produced over the years, a fine shot-stopper with a low error count.

Left: Sven-Goran Eriksson chats with Steven Gerrard during a training session before England's game against Denmark.

PATH TO THE FINALS:

WINNER IN EUROPE GROUP 6

	P	W	D	L	F	A	PTS
ENGLAND	10	8	1	1	17	5	25
POLAND	10	8	0	2	27	9	24
AUSTRIA	10	4	3	3	15	12	15
N IRELAND	10	2	3	5	10	18	9
WALES	10	2	2	6	10	15	8
AZERBAIJAN	10	0	3	7	1	21	3

ENGLAND Winners: 1966

Key to England's hopes of glory

It is up front where perhaps the greatest hope lies. Eight years ago, the mercurial Michael Owen held us transfixed as he danced through Argentina's defence as a raw 18-year-old. With 35 international goals, plundered at a rate of almost one in two, Owen is as good as anyone playing on the shoulder of the last defender. The jewel in the crown, though, is Wayne Rooney. His explosive performances at Euro 2004 brought forth comparisons with Pele at Sweden '58. England became a shadow side when he limped out of the quarter-final clash with hosts Portugal. If he remains fit and the red mist is kept at bay, Rooney holds the key to England's hopes of World Cup glory.

The above represents Plan A. While the back-up plans have borne little fruit in recent years, Sven's first-choice XI will present formidable opposition to anyone in Germany – the excellent 3–2 victory over strongly-fancied Argentina last November bears witness to that. At an average age of 25, it will be the youngest England side to take the field in a World Cup, and, many believe, the strongest. The fact that they will not have to play in stultifying heat or draining humidity is another favourable factor. If the rub of the green goes their way, the boys of 2006 might just follow their 1966 counterparts into sporting immortality.

Above: Frank Lampard scores from the penalty spot against Austria during their World Cup qualifying match at Old Trafford.

Opposite: Michael Owen celebrates with David Beckham and Wayne Rooney after Owen scored against Argentina.

PARAGUAY FIFA ranking: 33 • World Cup history: 7th appearance

Olympic finalists aim for knockout stage

Paraguay reached the second round at the last two World Cups, losing to eventual winners France in 1998 and runners-up Germany four years ago, on both occasions by the odd goal. This time Paraguay qualified with a game to spare, though there had been a mixed bag of results along the way. The key was a nine-match run which produced just one defeat, and the highlight was undoubtedly the 1–0 victory over Argentina, Paraguay's first win over that country in a World Cup qualifier. The inconsistency bred frustration among the fans, though Uruguayan coach Anibal Ruiz survived, one of only three men to keep his job for the duration of the campaign.

Goalkeeper and talisman Jose Luis Chilavert has finally gone; the new star between the sticks is Justo Villar, a renowned shot-stopper. Carlos Gamarra, who had a spell with Inter Milan, marshals the defence. Midfielders Julio Dos Santos and Edgar Barreto have established themselves in the side after impressing during Paraguay's run to the final at the Athens Olympics. Up front Ruiz has some exciting options. Bayern Munich's Roque Santa Cruz is still there, while Jose Cardozo's seven goals put him joint-second in the CONMEBOL zone's list of hotshots. Then there's the exciting Nelson Haedo Valdez, who scored the goal in Venezuela which secured qualification.

Paraguay has lost both its previous matches against England: 3–0 in the second round at Mexico '86, 4–0 in a friendly at Anfield in 2002. Sweden, also playing in their home continent, should prove too strong for Paraguay, who will struggle to reach the knockout stage this time.

STAR PLAYER
Nelson Haedo Valdez
D.O.B. 28 November 1983

Werder Bremen chairman Jurgen Born went to watch Nelson Haedo Valdez after hearing rave reviews about his performances in 2000–01, even though it was only at amateur level. He was impressed enough to invite the 18-year-old to Germany for a trial. Haedo Valdez was promoted to the first team in 2003, and a year later Werder Bremen were celebrating a domestic double.

His first taste of tournament football came in the 2004 World Youth Championship, where he scored against a Germany side that included a couple of team-mates. He played in Paraguay's run to the quarter-final at the 2004 Copa America tournament, but was frustrated at being unable to make a dent in the Jose Cardozo-Roque Santa Cruz strike partnership for the World Cup qualifiers. He went public, pointing out that he was the only Paraguayan – Santa Cruz apart – playing in the Champions League and merited a place in the squad. The risky strategy paid off, and he was soon part of Anibal Ruiz's set-up.

PATH TO THE FINALS:

FOURTH IN SOUTH AMERICAN GROUP

	P	W	D	L	F	A	PTS
BRAZIL	18	9	7	2	35	17	34
ARGENTINA	18	10	4	4	29	17	34
ECUADOR	18	8	4	6	23	19	28
PARAGUAY	18	8	4	6	23	23	28
URUGUAY	18	6	7	5	23	28	25
COLOMBIA	18	6	6	6	24	16	24
CHILE	18	5	7	6	18	22	22
VENEZUELA	18	5	3	10	20	28	18
PERU	18	4	6	8	20	28	18
BOLIVIA	18	4	2	12	20	37	14

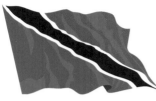

Soca Warriors on the march

Halfway through the qualifying campaign, Trinidad and Tobago's hopes looked slim as they took just four points from their first five games. It took the arrival of former Real Madrid coach Leo Beenhakker to put the team on track. Three successive victories, including a 2–1 win over Mexico, lifted the side to fourth spot and a play-off against Bahrain. Port Vale midfielder Chris Birchall earned the Soca Warriors a 1–1 draw at home with a 30-yard screamer, and Wrexham defender Dennis Lawrence headed in a Dwight Yorke corner for the only goal of the return. A national holiday was declared at home.

Dwight Yorke is the star name, though strike partner Stern John top-scored with 12 goals, putting him second in the list of CONCACAF marksmen. Most of the squad are based in Britain, though apart from Falkirk's Russell Latapy, West Ham's Shaka Hislop and Rangers' defender Marvin Andrews, they are plying their trade at the lower levels.

Wiith a population of less than 1.5 million, Trinidad and Tobago is the smallest nation ever to participate in the finals, but the Soca Warriors' motto is 'Believe in the impossible'. Paraguay looks to be their best hope of a positive result, but it is stretching credulity to breaking point to think that the team can cause an upset against England or Sweden.

STAR PLAYER
Dwight Yorke
D.O.B. 3 November 1971

When Dwight Yorke swapped the Premiership for Sydney United last year, he seemed to be following the well-worn path of many superstars: winding down his career in pleasant climes and a less demanding league. The World Cup has propelled the former treble-winning Red Devil back into the limelight, and given him the chance to fulfil his one remaining ambition.

Yorke was spotted by Graham Taylor when the latter's Aston Villa side was on tour in the West Indies. He paid just £120,000 to bring Yorke to Villa Park, one of the shrewdest deals of the modern era.

Alex Ferguson broke Manchester United's transfer record when he paid £12 million for Yorke in August 1998. The striker immediately formed a devastating partnership with Andy Cole, the duo providing the firepower which took United to the famous treble in Yorke's debut season. Yorke contributed 29 goals and picked up the Player of the Year award.

He spent three more seasons at United, but by 2002 he was out of favour at Old Trafford, and also failed to spark in spells with Blackburn and Birmingham.

Yorke came out of retirement to help the Soca Warriors qualify for Germany. The honour of captaining his country in its first World Cup adventure might just be the catalyst for him to recapture his best form.

PATH TO THE FINALS:

FOURTH IN CONCACAF FINAL QUALIFYING GROUP

	P	W	D	L	F	A	PTS
USA	10	7	1	2	16	6	22
MEXICO	10	7	1	2	22	9	22
COSTA RICA	10	5	1	4	15	14	16
TRINIDAD & TOBAGO	10	4	1	5	10	15	13
GUATEMALA	10	3	2	5	16	18	11
PANAMA	10	0	2	8	4	21	2

SWEDEN FIFA ranking: 15 • World Cup history: 11th appearance

England's nemesis for 38 years

Sweden was the surprise winner of the Group of Death in Japan and Korea four years ago, coming out on top of the pile over England, Argentina and Nigeria before going down to a Senegal golden goal in the last 16. The Swedes were group winners again at Euro 2004, albeit on goal difference ahead of Denmark and Italy, and only missed out on a semi-final berth when they lost on penalties against Holland.

This time round, the Swedes won eight of their ten matches, including fine doubles over Bulgaria and Hungary. Croatia also dropped six points, but topped the group thanks to the 1–0 home and away victories they scored over Lars Lagerback's team. Second place and 24 points was good enough for automatic qualification.

Sweden once again came out of the hat with England. Statisticians trawled through the record books to discover that Sweden hadn't lost to England since May 1968, when the reigning world champions ran out 3–1 winners at Wembley. Paraguay is ranked much lower, and with the minnows of Trinidad and Tobago fleshing out Group B, Sweden should have little trouble reaching the knockout stage again.

Sweden has strength all over the pitch, particularly going forward, where the twin-pronged threat of Zlatan Ibrahimovic and Henrik Larsson, backed up by the surging runs of Freddie Ljungberg, will trouble any defence. The fact that the Swedes averaged three goals a game in the qualifiers shows their offensive quality; only the Czech Republic and Portugal were able to boast a better goalscoring record than that. At the back, just four goals conceded in 15 hours of football speaks for itself.

It may well be that Sweden and England are both through to the last 16 by the time the sides meet in Cologne on 20 June. However, topping the group could be crucial, as the winners will face the runners-up in Germany's group, almost certainly Costa Rica, Ecuador or Poland. Second spot in Group B looks likely to lead to a meeting with the hosts in the second round, a less enticing proposition. The canny Lagerback will know that just as well as Sven, and he will therefore be doing his best to extend Sweden's unbeaten run over his compatriot's side.

SWEDEN

STAR PLAYER
Zlatan Ibrahimovic
D.O.B. 3 October 1981

Zlatan Ibrahimovic has had a reputation for being temperamental and difficult, though his talent has never been in doubt. Since moving to Juventus, the waywardness seems to have gone and Ibrahimovic has flourished in a league hardly known for being overly generous to strikers.

He was born to Bosnian immigrants in Malmo, joining the professional ranks with the club Nottingham Forest beat in the 1979 European Cup final. That was in 1999. Arsene Wenger was said to have been interested in signing him, but Leo Beenhakker – now coaching Trinidad and Tobago – brokered the deal which took him to Ajax in 2001.

Over the next three years he established himself in the Ajax side, particularly under Ronald Koeman. In an injury-hit 2003–04 he still managed 13 goals in 16 games to help Ajax wrest the league title back from PSV. That summer, Juve came calling and Ibrahimovic departed to Turin in a £13 million deal. 16 goals in a championship-winning debut campaign made him the fans' choice as player of the season. He was nominated for 2005 World Player of the Year, and also picked up Sweden's domestic award.

Ibrahimovic made his tournament debut by making the squad for Japan and Korea, having won his first cap the year before, aged 19. By Euro 2004 he was a first choice striker, forming a potent partnership with Henrik Larsson in Sweden's run to the last eight. He was on target against Bulgaria and Italy.

Eight goals in the qualifying campaign put him third in the Euro zone's list of marksmen, behind Pauleta and Jan Koller. Germany could be the stage where the 24-year-old takes world football by the scruff of the neck, and if he and Larsson are on song up front, Sweden have the resilience to pose a threat to any opponents.

Opposite: Sweden's Kim Kallstrom, 2nd right, celebrates with team-mates Henrik Larsson, left, Freddie Ljungberg, 2nd left, and Marcus Allback, right.

PATH TO THE FINALS:

RUNNER-UP IN EUROPE GROUP 8

	P	W	D	L	F	A	PTS
CROATIA	10	7	3	0	21	5	24
SWEDEN	10	8	0	2	30	4	24
BULGARIA	10	4	3	3	17	17	15
HUNGARY	10	4	2	4	13	14	14
ICELAND	10	1	1	8	14	26	4
MALTA	10	0	3	7	4	28	3

Group C

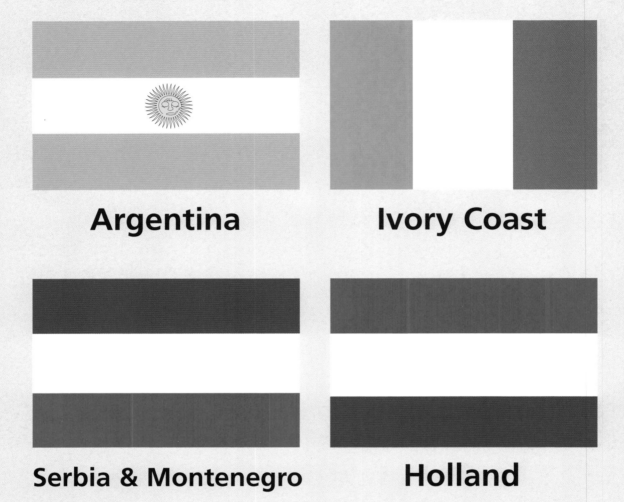

Argentina   **Ivory Coast**

Serbia & Montenegro   **Holland**

Saturday June 10 Hamburg
Argentina v Ivory Coast

Sunday June 11 Leipzig
Serbia & Montenegro v Holland

Friday June 16 Gelsenkirchen and Stuttgart
Argentina v Serbia & Montenegro, Holland v Ivory Coast

Wednesday June 21 Frankfurt and Munich
Holland v Argentina, Ivory Coast v Serbia & Montenegro

ARGENTINA FIFA ranking: 4 • World Cup history: 14th appearance

Qualification at a canter

Argentina booked its place in Germany at a relative canter, with three matches to spare. The game that secured the team's place in the finals was an impressive 3–1 home victory against Brazil in June 2005. A brace from Chelsea's Hernan Crespo and a terrific 25-yard left-foot drive from Juan Riquelme put the home side 3–0 up and left Brazil looking down the barrel of their worst result since the defeat by the same margin against France in the 1998 World Cup final. A late Roberto Carlos free kick salvaged some pride, but it was still an emphatic result.

With one game to play, Argentina headed the CONMEBOL group, three points clear of their arch-rivals. A surprise 1–0 away defeat to also-rans Uruguay allowed the five-time World Cup winners to pip them in the final table, though the stats from the 18-match marathon series suggest that there is precious little between the two South American giants. Brazil reversed the 3–1 scoreline when the teams met in Belo Horizonte, and both sides went down in the rarefied atmosphere of Quito, Ecuador running out 2–0 winners against Argentina. Jose Pekerman's side won 10 games – one more than Brazil – but there was a defeat in Paraguay as well as Uruguay; Brazil's 3–0 home win over Venezuela in their final game meant that Argentina slipped to second place on goal difference.

News from the Argentina camp since qualification was clinched has been mixed. At last summer's Confederations Cup, the team reached the final with a shoot-out victory over Mexico, but then crashed 4–1 to Brazil. Last November, Argentina were 2–1 up with minutes to go in their Geneva friendly against England, when Michael Owen turned the game around with two late headers.

By then, Pekerman was already contemplating going to Germany without attacking full-back Gabriel Heinze, who sustained cruciate ligament damage in Manchester United's Champions League match against Villareal in September. Defender Roberto Ayala, who missed the 2002 World Cup through injury, also had a knee problem requiring surgery, though he is expected to be fit for the finals. Ayala and Javier Zanetti, with 200 caps between them, are both veterans of France '98.

ARGENTINA Winners 1978, 1986

No slip-ups this time

Pekerman seems to have caught the 'tinker man' bug. He has tried over 50 players since he took the reins in October 2004, many of those given an opportunity and discarded at a dizzying rate. That hasn't made for stability, though there are a few names guaranteed to feature in the first-choice XI: Hernan Crespo, joint-second top scorer behind Ronaldo in the qualifiers, looks set to spearhead the attack; Juan Roman Riquelme, whose silky playmaking skills were much in evidence in the defeat by England, will pull the strings; and in Lionel Messi, Argentina seems to have unearthed a player worthy to inherit the Maradona mantle.

Argentina can count itself a mite unlucky to be drawn in the Group of Death for the second tournament running. Four years ago, the two-time champions made a shock first-round exit, losing out to Sweden and England; it was the first time in eight World Cups that Argentina had failed to progress beyond the group stage, a record dating back to 1974.

Pekerman will want no slip-ups this time, though the competition is stiff. Holland eliminated Argentina at the quarter-final stage at France '98, Dennis Begkamp hitting a sublime winner. The present Dutch side looks ominously strong, and Argentina also has to contend with Ivory Coast – this year's African Cup of Nations runners-up – and a dangerous Serbia and Montenegro side which looks as secure as the Bank of England at the back.

PATH TO THE FINALS:

RUNNER-UP IN SOUTH AMERICAN GROUP

	P	W	D	L	F	A	PTS
BRAZIL	18	9	7	2	35	17	34
ARGENTINA	18	10	4	4	29	17	34
ECUADOR	18	8	4	6	23	19	28
PARAGUAY	18	8	4	6	23	23	28
URUGUAY	18	6	7	5	23	28	25
COLOMBIA	18	6	6	6	24	16	24
CHILE	18	5	7	6	18	22	22
VENEZUELA	18	5	3	10	20	28	18
PERU	18	4	6	8	20	28	18
BOLIVIA	18	4	2	12	20	37	14

Above: England's Frank Lampard and Argentina's Juan Roman Riquelme battle for the ball.

ARGENTINA

STAR PLAYER

Juan Roman Riquelme

D.O.B. 26 June 1978

Jose Pekerman sees a lot of Zinedine Zidane in Juan Roman Riquelme, and has high hopes that his playmaker will do for Argentina in 2006 what Zidane did for France eight years ago.

Riquelme was on the books of Argentinos Juniors as a youngster but at 17 he was snapped up by Boca Juniors, the club he had supported as a boy. Riquelme spent seven years with Boca, during which time the club twice won the Copa Libertadores. On the second of those occasions, in 2001, Riquelme was named South American Footballer of the Year.

The following year he joined Barcelona, a team then in a transitional phase. Real Madrid, Valencia and Deportivo la Coruna were all outperforming Barca, and Riquelme struggled with the pressure of trying to restore the club to pre-eminence. Overshadowed by another new signing, Ronaldinho, Riquelme failed to secure a regular place and was loaned to Villarreal. Three years on, Barca must be regretting allowing him to slip through their fingers. Riquelme's form was instrumental in Villareal qualifying for their first Champions League campaign this season, the team's scalps including both Everton and Manchester United. Riquelme's form earned him a nomination for the 2005 World Player of the Year award.

ARGENTINA

STAR PLAYER

Hernan Crespo

D.O.B. 5 July 1975

When Hernan Crespo scored twice in AC Milan's scintillating first-half performance against Liverpool in the 2005 Champions League final, he must have thought he had sealed victory for the club he had joined on loan from Chelsea the previous summer. Liverpool's memorable comeback prevented that, and Crespo had to be content with a losers medal, and outshining Shevchenko in the showpiece of European club football.

From his days as a teenager with River Plate, Crespo has always been a prolific goalscorer. He got his international call-up at 19, and two years later, in 1996, helped River Plate win the Copa Libertadores, the continent's club championship. His two goals in the second leg of the final turned the tie against America de Cali around. That summer he signed for Serie A club Parma, where he spent four productive years. In 1999 he opened the scoring in Parma's 3–0 win over Marseille in the UEFA Cup final.

In 2000, Crespo became the world's most expensive player when Lazio paid £36 million to acquire his services. In 2000–01 he was the league's top marksman, taking over from Milan's Shevchenko. Financial pressures forced Lazio to sell their goal machine in 2002, Inter Milan glad to find a top-class replacement for Real Madrid-bound Ronaldo.

A year later, he was on the move again, this time to Stamford Bridge in a £16.8 million deal. He took time to adjust to the demands of the Premiership, and after a disappointing campaign, incoming Chelsea boss Jose Mourinho sanctioned a season-long loan deal back to Italy. Crespo was keen to stay on at Milan, but Mourinho persuaded him to return to Stamford Bridge last summer.

He has tended to stand behind the powerfully-built Didier Drogba in the Chelsea pecking order, yet by common consensus, Crespo is the superior finisher. Seven goals in the qualifiers put him joint-second behind Ronaldo in the list of South American hotshots. Two of those came in the 3–1 victory over Brazil in Buenos Aires: one a sweet drive from distance, the other a near-post header. Five months later, in the 3–2 defeat by England in Geneva, Crespo notched his 29th goal in his 52nd appearance for Argentina, a strike rate which few international strikers can match.

ARGENTINA

STAR PLAYER

Lionel Messi

D.O.B. 24 June 1987

Jose Pekerman is desperately trying to dampen the hype surrounding wunderkind Lionel Messi, the man being hailed as the new Maradona. Although Messi plays his club football in the goldfish bowl of the Nou Camp, Pekerman has done all he can to take the spotlight off the young star in the international arena. He was a regular squad member in the qualifiers but barely used; and the decision not to play him in the high-profile friendly against England last November appears to have been a deliberate attempt to keep him under wraps until the action proper gets under way.

Messi came to prominence with Newell's Old Boys, whose coach, Enrique Domínguez, knew that here was a special talent. 'He could do things with a ball that defied the laws of physics. The only other person I have ever seen do that was Diego Maradona.'

The family planned to move to Spain, where better wages would finance the treatment Messi needed for a hormone deficiency. The 13-year-old Messi stood just 1m 40cm tall when he arrived in his new country, yet Barcelona knew all about his precocious gifts and stepped in to pay the medical bills.

Messi made his Primera Liga debut as a 17-year-old in the 2004–05 season, becoming Barca's youngest ever scorer as the Catalan team won its first championship for six years. He then led Argentina to victory at the FIFA World Youth Championship, where he top-scored with six goals – including two in the 2–1 win over Nigeria in the final – and was named player of the tournament.

Spain's footballing officials had harboured hopes that Messi might opt to play for his adopted country. The awarding of Spanish citizenship gave him that option, but he has now won his international spurs with Argentina; and Pekerman will be less shy about unleashing him when the action gets under way in earnest in June.

IVORY COAST   FIFA ranking: 32 • World Cup history: First appearance

Drogba leads African challenge

Ivory Coast has reached the World Cup for the first time in eight attempts, after cashing in on a slip-up by five-time finalists Cameroon. The Indomitable Lions went into the final round a point clear at the top of the group, but managed only a 1–1 home draw against Egypt, missing from the penalty spot deep into injury time. Ivory Coast won 3–1 in Sudan, rendering the two head-to-head defeats by Cameroon irrelevant.

Chelsea's Didier Drogba, along with Gunners duo Kolo Toure and Emmanuel Eboue, are Ivory Coast's best known players, but virtually all the squad members turn out for European club sides. St Etienne midfielder Didier Zokora is one to watch.

On the eve of the African Cup of Nations the team lost Lens striker Aruna Dindane, who had just learned of the death of his baby daughter. Dindane hit six goals in the qualifiers, and his partnership with Drogba – who weighed in with 9 – was pivotal in Ivory Coast's campaign.

Perhaps the most important member of the team is Henri Michel, who coached France in the mid-'80s. Michel had a disastrous USA '94 with Cameroon, but his experience will be vital as the Ivory Coast enters unknown waters. Up to now, the 'Elephants' only claim to fame is their 1992 victory in the Cup of Nations, but many pundits are tipping them as dark horses. They are up against powerhouses Argentina and Holland, but Ivory Coast could well mount the strongest African challenge.

STAR PLAYER

Didier Drogba

D.O.B. 11 March 1978

Didier Drogba admitted that he underperformed in his debut season of Premiership football, despite the fact that Chelsea blew away the opposition in a record-breaking campaign. He got his second term away with a bang, scoring both goals in Chelsea's 2–1 win over Arsenal in the Community Shield curtain-raiser. Despite Hernan Crespo's return from a loan spell at AC Milan, Drogba maintained his position as the club's number one striker.

Drogba started out as a defender, and it wasn't until he reached his mid-20s that he arrived on the European stage as an ace marksman. That was in 2003–04 at Marseille, who had bought him on the strength of a fine season with Championnat strugglers Guingamp. He hit 11 goals in Marseille's Champions League and UEFA Cup campaigns, defeat to Valencia in the final of the latter competition mitigated by the Player of the Year award – and a £24 million move to Stamford Bridge.

Some commentators believe Crespo is the better finisher, but Drogba's power and pace makes him a thorn in the flesh of opposing defenders. Perhaps the best answer to the critics is the fact that Mourinho, with his bottomless purse, appears more than satisfied with the return on his investment.

PATH TO THE FINALS:

WINNER IN AFRICA GROUP 3

	P	W	D	L	F	A	PTS
IVORY COAST	10	7	1	2	20	7	22
CAMEROON	10	6	3	1	18	10	21
EGYPT	10	5	2	3	26	15	17
LIBYA	10	3	3	4	8	10	12
SUDAN	10	1	3	6	2	22	6
BENIN	10	1	2	7	9	23	5

SERBIA & MONTENEGRO   FIFA ranking: 47 • First appearance

Europe's meanest defence

Following the dismemberment of Yugoslavia in the early 90s, and the founding of Croatia, Bosnia, Macedonia and Slovenia as independent states, Serbia and Montenegro was the remaining political entity. It continued to compete as Yugoslavia until Euro 2004, when the country's FA adopted the new name.

Serbia and Montenegro failed to reach Portugal, finishing behind Italy and Wales in the qualifiers. This time it was a very different story. Not only did the team complete its programme unbeaten, but the 1–1 draw in Spain was the only game in which 'keeper Dragoslav Jervic had to pick the ball out of the net, the best defensive record of the Euro zone. The final game pitted them against Bosnia-Herzegovina, a potential powder-keg which could have seen the latter leapfrog their Balkan rivals for top spot. A Mateja Kezman goal settled the issue.

Spain's superstars were consigned to the play-offs, while Belgium, who gave Brazil a good run for their money in Japan and Korea, missed out completely.

Apart from Kezman, other familiar faces include Sasa Ilic, the former Charlton, West Ham and Portsmouth midfielder, now with Galatasaray, and ex-Villa striker Savo Milosevic, currently with Primera Liga side Osasuna. It also boasts Nemanja Vidic, whose superb defensive displays for Spartak Moscow as well as his country persuaded Sir Alex Ferguson to part with £7 million in January.

The big guns of Argentina and Holland are favourites to progress in this year's 'Group of Death', but they will not relish playing against Serbia and Montenegro. Ilija Petkovic was sanguine after the draw. 'This is a group of four excellent teams and there should be some great matches. Perhaps it should be called the Group of Joy.'

STAR PLAYER
Mateja Kezman
D.O.B. 12 April 1979

Mateja Kezman's bit-part contribution in Chelsea's title-winning campaign was a blot on an otherwise impressive cv. He scored goals by the sackful in his native Serbia, and particularly during his four-year spell in Holland. Kezman also made a promising start with Atletico Madrid, the club which ended his Premiership nightmare last summer.

He first took the eye with Partizan Belgrade, ending the 1999–2000 season as the country's top marksman. It wasn't enough to prevent the title going to Red Star, but it did earn him a move to PSV Eindhoven. The Dutch side needed to replace Old Trafford-bound Ruud van Nistelrooy, and over the next four years Kezman filled his boots admirably, scoring 105 goals in 122 league appearances and helping PSV win two championships. He was Dutch football's hotshot in three of the four seasons, and even in 2001–02, when Feyenoord's Pierre van Hooijdonk took top honours, Kezman returned a highly respectable 15 goals from 27 outings.

PATH TO THE FINALS:

WINNER EUROPE GROUP 7

	P	W	D	L	F	A	PTS
SERBIA & MONTENEGRO	10	6	4	0	16	1	22
SPAIN	10	5	5	0	19	3	20
BOSNIA-HERZEGOVINA	10	4	4	2	12	9	16
BELGIUM	10	3	3	4	16	11	12
LITHUANIA	10	2	4	4	8	9	10
SAN MARINO	10	0	0	10	2	40	0

HOLLAND FIFA ranking: 3 • World Cup history: 8th appearance

Dutch masters in hot form

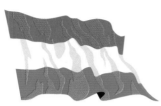

Marco van Basten, three times winner of the European Footballer of the Year award, was at the height of his powers when the Dutch claimed their only success in a major tournament, at Euro '88. 18 years on, van Basten aims to go one better as coach, drawing a line under the country's reputation for failing to live up to its billing when it really matters. In the past, overlarge egos have sometimes been a problem, leading to internal squabbles. Edgar Davids was sent home from Euro '96 following a spat with Guus Hiddink; and in 2003 Ruud van Nistelrooy was dropped after a run-in with Dick Advocaat during the Euro 2004 qualifiers.

On other occasions fortune has not favoured the Dutch. The 'Total Football' played by the 1970s side made Holland the team of the era, yet they finished on the losing side in consecutive World Cup finals. Their best effort since then came at France '98, where a sublime Dennis Bergkamp goal beat Argentina in the quarters, before the team went out on penalties to Brazil in the last four.

The Dutch missed out on Japan and Korea, trailing home third in their qualifying group, behind Portugal and the Republic of Ireland. There were no such slip-ups this time. Ten wins and two draws was the most emphatic qualifying campaign of the European zone, and all the more impressive as their group included the Czech Republic – ranked second in the world – and Romania, who reached the last eight in 1994. The Netherlands did the double over both, dropping points only in the two games against minnows Macedonia. However, they were already assured of top spot when the teams played out a goalless draw in Holland in the final group match.

The fact that Davids, Seedorf, Kluivert, Makaay and Hasselbaink may well find themselves surplus to requirements is an indication that the Dutch production line is churning out talent as remorselessly as ever. Arjen Robben, Robin van Persie, Wesley Sneijder and Rafael van der Vaart – who left Ajax for Hamburg last summer – represent the new breed. With the sizeable frame of veteran 'keeper Edwin van der Sar still filling the goal, and his United teammate van Nistelrooy on the goal trail up front, the Dutch once again have the potential to go a long way in the tournament.

Holland's failure to make the 2002 finals was the main reason why they were unseeded this time round. They were the team everyone wanted to avoid, and when Argentina, Ivory Coast and Serbia and Montenegro came out of the hat to join them in Group C, it was quickly nominated as this tournament's 'Group of Death'. The Oranje and South Americans should go through, but then again, who predicted that Sweden would top the 2002 'Group of Death', with Argentina making a first-round exit?

PATH TO THE FINALS:

WINNER EUROPE GROUP 1

	P	W	D	L	F	A	PTS
NETHERLANDS	12	10	2	0	27	3	32
CZECH REPUBLIC	12	9	0	3	35	12	27
ROMANIA	12	8	1	3	20	10	25
FINLAND	12	5	1	6	21	19	16
MACEDONIA	12	2	3	7	11	24	9
ARMENIA	12	1	1	10	3	25	4
ANDORRA	12	1	1	10	6	28	4

HOLLAND Runners-up: 1974, 1978

Above: Holland players celebrate with goalscorer Ryan Babel during a friendly against Italy.
Opposite: Holland coach Marco van Basten.

HOLLAND

Arjen Robben

D.O.B. 23 January 1984

By the tender age of 21 Arjen Robben's cv already included championship winners' medals for both the Dutch and English leagues. The flying winger helped PSV Eindhoven lift the Dutch title in his first term with the club, 2002–03; two years later he repeated that feat in the Premiership with Chelsea, having enhanced his reputation as one of Europe's most exciting young talents along the way.

Robben began his career with his home-town club Bedum, joining FC Groningen for the 2000–01 season. Groningen had just won promotion back to the top flight, and finished in the lower reaches of the table that year. 16-year-old Robben impressed, though, notably with a dazzling debut against league leaders Feyenoord. At the end of that campaign the deal to take him to PSV was done, but deferred for a year to give the player the chance to gain more experience and develop physically. In the title-winning season, in which PSV edged Ajax by one point, Robben hit 12 goals in 33 games, his superb form earning him the country's Young Player of the Year award.

Robben made his senior international debut against Portugal in April 2003. A year later the same opposition ended Holland's hopes of winning the European Championship. The hosts came out on top in their semi-final clash, but Robben could be more than satisfied with his contribution. He shone in the 3–0 group win over Latvia, and the team was 2–0 up and cruising against the Czech Republic when coach Dick Advocaat substituted him. Holland lost 3–2 but still progressed, Robben scoring the decisive penalty in the quarter-final shoot-out against Sweden.

By that time, Manchester United was chasing his signature. United offered in the region of £5 million, well below PSV's valuation, and in July Robben moved to Stamford Bridge for more than double that amount.

His debut season for the Blues was blighted by injury, but when he did make it onto the pitch the Chelsea faithful saw the kind of dazzling wing play reminiscent of a young Ryan Giggs. With his searing pace, marvellous control and perfect balance, Robben at full tilt is a joy to behold – unless you are an opposing defender, that is.

HOLLAND

STAR PLAYER

Ruud van Nistelrooy
D.O.B. 1 July 1976

Any defender set to face Ruud van Nistelrooy would be well advised not to examine his career stats too closely, assuming they want to get a good night's sleep. He has topped the scoring charts in Holland and the Premiership; stands third in the all-time European Cup-Champions League list, behind Raul and di Stefano, with 43 goals from 54 matches; and for good measure has banged in a goal every other game at international level.

One of the most prolific marksmen of the modern era began his career as a midfielder at Den Bosch, a Second Division side in the Dutch league. Heerenveen recognised a raw talent and gave the 21-year-old his chance in the Eredivisie, Holland's top division, and also converted him to a striker. A year later, in 1998, Bobby Robson paid £4.2 million to take him to PSV Eindhoven, the deal being done on van Nistelrooy's 22nd birthday.

He was the league's top scorer for the next two seasons, by which time he had attracted the attention of Sir Alex Ferguson. His value had rocketed to £19 million, though the transfer was delayed a year due to a cruciate ligament injury.

In his five years at Old Trafford, van Nistelrooy has continued scoring at a phenomenal rate. In his second season, 2002–2003, he hit a Premiership best 25 goals as United won the title yet again. In February 2004, less than three years after joining the club, he reached the century mark for the club. Two years later, he was within sight of his 150th, amassed from barely 200 outings in a United shirt.

Twenty-two goals in 44 appearances for Holland puts him ninth in the country's all-time list. The man immediately in his sights is his international manager, the great Marco van Basten, whose 24 goals came from 14 more matches. No doubt the 1992 World Footballer of the Year will be more than happy to see his star striker leapfrog him in the table and disappear into the distance during the World Cup.

Group D

Mexico

Iran

Angola

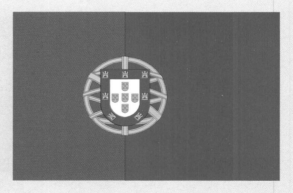

Portugal

Sunday June 11 Nuremberg and Cologne
Mexico v Iran, Angola v Portugal

Friday June 16 Hanover
Mexico v Angola

Saturday June 17 Frankfurt
Portugal v Iran

Wednesday June 21 Gelsenkirchen and Leipzig
Portugal v Mexico, Iran v Angola

MEXICO FIFA ranking: 6 • World Cup history: 13th appearance

The 67-goal seeds

The tortuous path to Germany for the CONCACAF contenders meant that the teams had to play 18 matches in total. Although some of Mexico's early opposition – including St Vincent and the Grenadines, and St Kitts and Nevis – wasn't the strongest, Ricardo Lavolpe's team still banged in 67 goals in all, the best record of any of the 31 qualifiers. The standard of the opposition at last summer's Confederations Cup, also staged in Germany, was considerably higher, and Mexico acquitted itself extremely well. The team topped a group including Brazil, Japan and Greece, beating the World Cup favourites 1–0. In the semis they fought a 120-minute 1–1 draw with South America's other traditional powerhouse, Argentina, before going down 6–5 in a shoot-out.

Mexico's Argentine coach likes to play an attacking game, making full use of the considerable striking talent he has at his disposal. Jaime Lozano, Francisco Fonseca and Jared Borgetti, hit 35 goals between them en route to the finals; they occupied three of the top five places in the list of CONCACAF hotshots. Had the group been decided on goal difference, Mexico would have finished on top; in the event, the USA's better head-to-head record gave Bruce Arena's side the edge.

Defender Claudio Suarez, dubbed 'The Emperor', won his 173rd cap in a friendly victory over Hungary in December 2005, equalling the world record set by Saudi Arabia 'keeper Mohammed Al-Deayea. Should Suarez make a mistake, opponents still have to find a way past Oswaldo Sanchez. The Chivas of Guadalajara 'keeper was in sparkling form at the Confederations Cup, and picked the ball out of his net just 10 times in 27 hours during the qualifiers. Sanchez aims to be the first Mexican 'keeper to make a name for himself in European club football, and will thus be keen to use the World Cup to showcase his skills.

This will be Mexico's 13th World Cup quest. Of the finalists, only Brazil, Germany, Italy and Argentina have a better record than that. The country enjoyed home advantage for its best efforts to date, reaching the quarter-finals in 1970 and 1986. As one of the seeds, 'El Tricolor' ought to emulate that achievement this time round, though it is generally agreed that they are the weakest of that top eight. The draw seemed favourable, though, with Iran and Angola on paper looking the most vulnerable in Group D. Mexico should at least make the last 16, along with Euro 2004 runners-up Portugal.

MEXICO

STAR PLAYER

Jared Borgetti
D.O.B. 14 August 1973

When Jared Borgetti, star striker for Pachuca and Mexico, announced last summer that he wanted to parade his skills on the European stage, Sam Allardyce quickly stumped up the £1 million fee to bring yet another accomplished international to the Reebok for a bargain price. By mid-season Borgetti had notched five goals but was frustrated over the lack of starts he was getting, and concerned that the lack of opportunity at club level might have a negative impact on his and Mexico's World Cup aspirations.

The man known to his army of fans as El Zorro del Desierto – The Desert Fox – had no peer when it came to finding the net during the qualifiers; his 14-goal haul put him top of the tree. Five of those came in the 8–0 aggregate drubbing of St Vincent and the Grenadines in the second group stage. Borgetti was also on target in the final-phase match against arch-rivals the USA at the Azteca Stadium, a game El Tricolor won 2–1.

The 32-year-old was on top form at last year's Confederations Cup, where he netted three times in Mexico's run to the semi-finals. One of those came against Brazil, his neat glancing header enough to beat the reigning world champions. Borgetti followed that up with a brace in the 4–0 win over Guatemala in the group stage of the CONCACAF Gold Cup. Although Mexico lost to Colombia in the quarters of that competition, Borgetti had the consolation of becoming Mexico's all-time leading scorer.

PATH TO THE FINALS:

RUNNER-UP IN CONCACAF FINAL QUALIFYING GROUP

	P	W	D	L	F	A	PTS
USA	10	7	1	2	16	6	22
MEXICO	10	7	1	2	22	9	22
COSTA RICA	10	5	1	4	15	14	16
TRINIDAD & TOBAGO	10	4	1	5	10	15	13
GUATEMALA	10	3	2	5	16	18	11
PANAMA	10	0	2	8	4	21	2

IRAN FIFA ranking: 22 • World Cup history: 3rd appearance

International goalscoring record

Iran had little trouble in reaching its third finals. Jordan, Qatar and Laos were overcome comfortably enough in the first phase, though Jordan did inflict a surprise 1–0 home defeat on Branko Ivankovic's side. Iran and Japan were the two big guns in Group B of the final round-robin, and they shared the honours with a victory apiece in the head-to-head meetings. Two dropped points away to Bahrain meant Iran had to settle for the runner-up spot, though both sides qualified with room to spare. The Croatian coach took much credit for a fine rebuilding job since the disappointing play-off defeat against the Republic of Ireland in 2002.

Skipper Ali Daei hit nine goals during the campaign, making him, unsurprisingly, the Asian zone's top scorer. However, the star of the show was playmaker Ali Karimi, whose sensational performances earned him the 2004 Asian Footballer of the Year award, and a dream move from UAE side Al-Ahli to Daei's former club, Bayern Munich. Striker Vahid Hashemian also played for the four-time European champions, picking up a Bundesliga winners medal in 2005 before joining rivals Hannover 96 last summer. Mehdi Mahdavikia is another who took the German route to furthering his career. He, too, is a former Asian Footballer of the Year, currently starring for SV Hamburg.

Six World Cup matches to date have produced just one victory, a 2–1 win over USA in 1998. Mahdavikia got on the scoresheet on that memorable day. The presence of Angola – ranked 43 places lower – in Group D should see that achievement doubled, but it is difficult to envisage Iran causing an upset against either Portugal or Mexico.

STAR PLAYER
Ali Daei
D.O.B. 21 March 1969

Ali Daei holds the world record for international goalscorers. In 2003, nine years after opening his account against Taipei, he notched his 85th goal for Iran, taking him one clear of Hungarian legend Ferenc Puskas and eight ahead of the immortal Pele. A year later, four goals against Laos in a World Cup qualifier took him past the century mark, his 102 goals coming in 133 appearances. With the ever-increasing competitiveness of international football, it is difficult to envisage this record being beaten.

Bayern Munich president Franz Beckenbauer was the prime mover in the deal a decade ago which took Daei from Arminia Bielefeld to Bayern Munich, and Daei subsequently became the first Asian player to feature in a Champions League match. Heavy international commitments, combined with the Bavarian club's star-studded squad, limited Daei's opportunities, but when he took the field he was regularly among the goals.

Daei also had a profitable spell with Hertha Berlin, before returning to his roots, and is currently winding down his career with Saba Battery in Tehran.

PATH TO THE FINALS:

RUNNER-UP IN ASIA GROUP B

	P	W	D	L	F	A	PTS
JAPAN	6	5	0	1	9	4	15
IRAN	6	4	1	1	7	3	13
BAHRAIN	6	1	1	4	4	7	4
NORTH KOREA	6	1	0	5	5	11	3

ANGOLA FIFA ranking: 60 • World Cup history: First appearance

Debut World Cup adventure

The lowest-ranked country of the 32 qualifiers made heavy weather of its pre-qualifier against Chad, squeezing through on away goals. But the team then hit the glory trail, coming out on top in a group including Nigeria, who had reached the last three World Cup finals and made it to the second round in 1994 and 1998.

It was a desperately close call, the teams having identical records as they went into the final round of matches, with the Super Eagles holding a far superior goal difference. Angola went to Rwanda knowing that victory wouldn't leave them sweating on the Nigeria-Zimbabwe result. The Super Eagles thrashed Zimbabwe 5–1, but Angola won too, courtesy of a late header by their inspirational captain Fabrice 'Akwa' Maieco. That preserved the status quo, and Angola's four points taken from the head-to-head meetings meant they were able to look forward to their first World Cup adventure. It was a marvellous achievement for a country racked by civil war for over a quarter of a century.

With Mexico the seeded side in Group D, and Iran also in the mix, Angola could scarcely bemoan its fortune in the draw. The team also meets Portugal, the league where many of the squad play their club football. Even so, anything other than wooden spoonists will represent a decent showing. Angola's cause wasn't helped in January, when star defender Yamba Asha – the only ever-present in the 12 qualifiers – received a nine-month ban for a doping offence.

STAR PLAYER

Fabrice 'Akwa' Maieco
D.O.B. 30 May 1977

It was Fabrice Akwa's 80th-minute header against Rwanda in Kigali which settled a nervy encounter and ensured that Angola would be heading for Germany at Nigeria's expense. Akwa is the veteran of the side, a survivor of Angola's only two African Cup of Nations forays prior to 2006. Those efforts, in 1996 and 1998, failed to produce a single victory, making the achievements of the past two years all the more remarkable.

Akwa may have lost a yard of pace, but his movement is clever and he remains the team's most influential player. His five-goal haul in the qualifiers – which also included the strike that secured a vital home victory over Nigeria – made him Angola's top marksman. By the end of the series he had notched over 30 international goals at around a goal every other game. Akwa is a crowd-pleaser and a hero to the Black Antelopes fans.

PATH TO THE FINALS:

WINNER IN AFRICA GROUP 4

	P	W	D	L	F	A	PTS
ANGOLA	10	6	3	1	12	6	21
NIGERIA	10	6	3	1	21	7	21
ZIMBABWE	10	4	3	3	13	14	15
GABON	10	2	4	4	11	13	10
ALGERIA	10	1	5	4	8	15	8
RWANDA	10	1	2	7	6	16	5

'The Brazil of Europe'

Few teams matched the form of Euro 2004 runners-up Portugal in the qualifying campaign for Germany. One of seven European countries to complete their programme unbeaten, Portugal found the back of the net 35 times, almost three goals per game. Only the Czech Republic equalled that tally, but Karel Bruckner's side lost three matches in the process. The Portuguese were also niggardly at the back, conceding just five times in 18 hours. That gave 'Big Phil' Scolari's side the best goal difference in Europe, and in Paris St-Germain striker Pauleta, who notched 11 goals along the way, the zone's most potent finisher. His haul took him past the legendary Eusebio's record of 41 goals for his country. This was by no means Europe's strongest group, but Portugal qualified at a canter and the statistics make impressive reading.

Ricardo Carvalho and Paulo Ferreira both picked up Champions League winners medals with Porto in 2003–04, and were early transfer targets when manager Jose Mourinho relocated to Stamford Bridge that summer. They were an integral part of a defensive unit that shipped just 15 league goals all season in winning the 2004–05 Premiership title.

Midfielder Tiago, who joined from Benfica at the same time as his compatriots, suffered from the rotation system and joined French champions Lyon after just one season at Chelsea. Tiago, Deco and Maniche – who arrived at Stamford Bridge in the January transfer window – form a powerful central axis. The latter pair were also graduates from the Porto class of 2004, though Deco was snapped up by Barcelona shortly after the famous 3–0 victory over Monaco.

No doubt Germany will witness a slew of step-overs from Cristiano Ronaldo, and though Luis Figo's footwork may not quite have the quicksilver quotient it once did, the last of Portugal's much-vaunted 'Golden Generation' may just have one last hurrah left in him.

Scolari, who led Brazil to victory in Japan and Korea, was unhappy that Portugal wasn't seeded for the finals. His spirits must have been lifted by a draw that pitted his side against Mexico – by common consent the weakest of FIFA's top eight countries – together with outsiders Iran and Angola. The country dubbed 'the Brazil of Europe' should have few problems in reaching the last 16, and will present a formidable obstacle to anyone at the knockout stage, as England and Holland found to their cost at Euro 2004.

PATH TO THE FINALS:

WINNERS EUROPE GROUP THREE

	P	W	D	L	F	A	PTS
PORTUGAL	12	9	3	0	35	5	30
SLOVAKIA	12	6	5	1	24	8	23
RUSSIA	12	6	5	1	23	12	23
ESTONIA	12	5	2	5	16	17	18
LATVIA	12	4	3	5	18	21	15
LIECHTENSTEIN	12	2	2	8	13	23	8
LUXEMBOURG	12	0	0	12	5	48	0

STAR PLAYER

Deco

D.O.B. 27 August 1977

Playmaker Anderson Luiz de Sousa – Deco, as he is better known – took the eye of fans throughout Europe with his man-of-the-match performance in the 2002–03 UEFA Cup final, when Porto beat Glasgow Celtic 3–2 in Seville. To Brazilian and Portuguese supporters he was already a known quantity. Deco played for Sao Paulo teams Nacional and Corinthians before joining Benfica as a 19-year-old, in 1997. The Lisbon club loaned him out to second division side Alverca, but on his return they couldn't agree terms and Deco moved to Salgueiros. His performances there took the eye of neighbours Porto, who signed him in the winter transfer window of 1998–99.

Porto missed out on the championship for the next three years, but Deco shone in this barren period. He earned a reputation for being abrasive – he had his share of yellow and red cards – but he was undoubtedly a midfield general to rival the best in Europe. Top performances were translated into silverware after Jose Mourinho's arrival. As well as playing a major part in Porto's UEFA Cup success, Deco was a key figure in the club's back-to-back league titles, and in the victorious Champions League campaign of 2003–04, culminating in the 3–0 win over Monaco in the final. Deco got on the scoresheet, and to put the icing on the cake he picked up UEFA's Most Valuable Player award.

When Mourinho moved to Stamford Bridge, he was soon spending some of Roman Abramovich's millions on his former Porto charges. Deco was rumoured to be on the verge of joining Chelsea, but long-time admirers Barcelona stepped in to get his signature. Six months later, in December 2004, Deco was named runner-up to Shevchenko in the European Footballer of the Year poll. And his first season at the Nou Camp yielded a championship medal, Barca's first La Liga title in six years.

Overlooked by Brazil's national team, Deco became eligible for Portugal under the residence rule, though his selection was not without controversy. He made his debut for Portugal In March 2003 – against Brazil – coming off the bench to score the winner from a 25-yard free kick. It was Portugal's first victory over Brazil since the group stage of the 1966 World Cup. It also helped to silence the critics, whose number had included Luis Figo.

Following the disappointment of defeat to Greece on home soil in the final of Euro 2004, the man Porto fans dubbed 'Magico' will be hoping his wizardry can help Portugal go one better in Germany.

PORTUGAL

Cristiano Ronaldo

D.O.B. 5 February 1985

As Manchester United fans came to terms with the loss of David Beckham to Real Madrid in the summer of 2003, they were no doubt keen to get the measure of the club's new signings. Attracting Kleberson, a World Cup winner with Brazil, was a coup; unveiling an 18-year-old from Sporting Lisbon at the same time probably slipped under the ordinary fan's radar. The footballing cognoscenti knew differently – as did the United players, who had been on the receiving end of some Ronaldo trickery in a pre-season friendly to mark the opening of Sporting's new stadium.

It is not difficult to judge which of those 2003 signings made the greater impact. The Brazilian was shipped off to Besiktas last summer; the Madeira-born Portuguese has added a cutting edge to his bewitching array of skills and at 21 is a global star. His £12 million move three years ago made him the most expensive teenager in British transfer history; even in today's more restrained market, that figure now looks like a steal.

Ronaldo won his first senior cap in 2003, and was a member of the side that marched to the final of the European Championship the following year. He scored against Greece in the opening group match – a game Portugal lost 2–1 – and was also on target in the 2–1 semi-final victory over Holland. That set up another meeting with Greece in the final, but the hosts were again beaten. Ronaldo's personal stock had risen, both from his performances at that tournament and for the starring role he played in The FA Cup final demolition of Millwall.

Ronaldo is not without his critics. Some claim his fancy footwork doesn't create enough goals, either for himself or his team-mates. Seven goals in the qualifiers – the second best in Europe – showed that he is addressing that issue. And even if the tricks don't always come off, Ronaldo will always be a refreshing antidote to the sterile play that can sometimes afflict a high-stakes match.

Group E

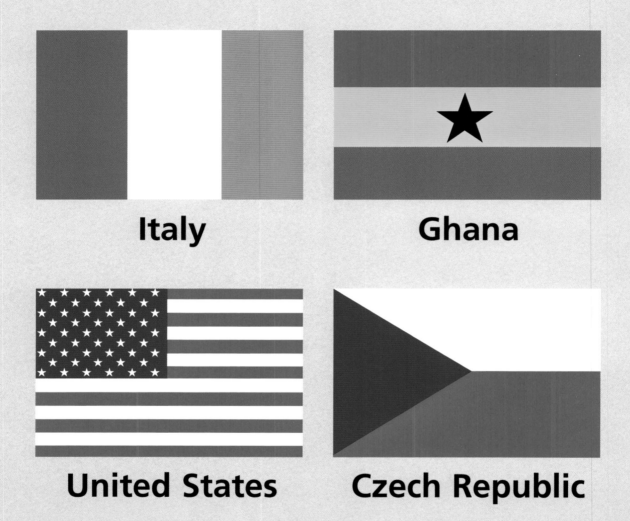

Italy

Ghana

United States

Czech Republic

Monday June 12 Hanover and Gelsenkirchen
Italy v Ghana, United States v Czech Republic

Saturday June 17 Kaiserslautern and Cologne
Italy v United States, Czech Republic v Ghana

Thursday June 22 Hamburg and Nuremberg
Czech Republic v Italy, Ghana v United States

ITALY FIFA ranking: 12 • World Cup history: 16th appearance

Azzurri hoping for better luck

With three victories and two appearances in the final to its credit, Italy has the third best World Cup record, behind Brazil and Germany. Germany 2006 will mark Italy's 16th appearance in the 18 finals held since the Jules Rimet Trophy was first contested in 1930. The Azzurri didn't take part in the inaugural tournament; Sweden '58 is thus the only World Cup to date for which Italy has failed to qualify.

The Italian side invariably goes into the major tournaments among the favourites, and Japan and Korea 2002 was no exception. Two years on from the agony of the Euro 2000 final, when Italy came within seconds of beating France, the team suffered further heartache. Italy was on the wrong end of some harsh decisions, and with better luck might have gone further than the second round, where they were beaten by a South Korea golden goal.

Marcello Lippi replaced Giovanni Trapattoni as Azzurri coach after further disappointment at Euro 2004, Italy this time failing to progress beyond the group stage. Once again the team had been somewhat unlucky; a win and two draws proved insufficient as Denmark and Sweden played out a 2–2 draw in their final match, a result which put them both through at Italy's expense.

Lippi, who won five Serie A titles and the Champions League in his two spells with Juventus, opted for a clean slate approach: even the biggest names were not guaranteed a place in the side, something Alessandro Del Piero and Christian Vieri soon found to their cost. A new generation of stars emerged, all eager to seize their opportunity during the Germany 2006 qualifiers. Cristian Zaccardo, Mauro Esposito and Alberto Gilardino were among those drafted into the side during the campaign. Gilardino and Fiorentina's Luca Toni formed a strike partnership capable of unnerving any defence. These young tyros, alongside established players such as Alessandro Nesta, Francesco Totti, Gianluca Zambrotta, Fabio Cannavaro and 'keeper Gianluigi Buffon, will make Italy formidable opponents in Germany. Del Piero, who was eventually restored to the side, was quick to praise the team ethic instilled into the squad by his former club boss.

ITALY Winners: 1934, 1938, 1982

Looking for victory no. 4

The road to the finals got off to a rocky start as Italy went behind to an early John Carew goal in their opening fixture, at home to Norway. The team recovered to win that game, Toni hitting a late winner. The only hiccup thereafter came in the surprise 1–0 defeat in Slovenia, though Belarus did give Lippi's men a fright by scoring three times in Parma before eventually capitulating 4–3.

Norway went on a six-match unbeaten run to become Italy's closest rivals for top spot. Kenny Miller's double in Oslo for a rejuvenated Scotland dealt the Scandinavian side's chances a mortal blow. Miller was also on target in the home match against Italy, but a Fabio Grosso goal earned the visitors a valuable point. Italy clinched qualification with a game to spare, courtesy of a Cristian Zaccardo strike which beat Slovenia in their penultimate fixture. Christian Vieri, ousted by Toni after the latter's sparkling hat-trick in the 4–1 win in Belarus, found himself back in favour and scored his first goal under Lippi in the final match of the campaign, a 2–1 win over Moldova.

Although Italy is one of the seeded countries, the draw pitted the Azzurri against two sides rated above them in the FIFA rankings. The Czech Republic was one of the second-line sides that everyone wanted to avoid, while Bruce Arena's USA are determined to at least match their quarter-final achievement of four years ago. A big name will be packing its bags when the Group E matches are complete; Italian fans will feel that if their team gets the slice of luck it is due, then a fourth World Cup success is a real possibility.

Above right: Fabio Grosso (facing) is congratulated by Andrea Pirlo on scoring an equaliser against Scotland.

PATH TO THE FINALS:

WINNER IN EUROPE GROUP 5

	P	W	D	L	F	A	PTS
ITALY	10	7	2	1	18	8	23
NORWAY	10	5	3	2	12	7	18
SCOTLAND	10	2	5	3	9	7	13
SLOVENIA	10	3	3	4	10	13	12
BELARUS	10	2	4	4	12	14	10
MOLDOVA	10	0	2	8	6	16	2

ITALY

STAR PLAYER

Alberto Gilardino

D.O.B. 5 July 1982

On the day that Paolo Rossi scored his famous World Cup hat-trick in the 3–2 victory over Brazil in Barcelona, a baby was born in Biella, northern Italy, who is well on the way to following in the footsteps of Riva, Rossi, Schillaci and Co.: Alberto Gilardino. Gilardino made his top-flight debut in January 2000, aged 17, for FC Piacenza. From the outset he showed all the attributes of a top striker: pace, a powerful shot with both feet and prowess in the air. He is no prima donna, though, always prepared to chase back and win the ball in midfield when necessary.

After a spell at Hellas Verona, Gilardino joined Parma, where his second season yielded an impressive 23 goals in 34 Serie A games. That put him second in the list of Italian hotshots, just one behind Andriy Shevchenko.

After another sparkling season with Parma in 2004–05, Gilardino became a teammate of the Ukrainian star, joining AC Milan in the summer in an £18 million deal. He was out of the blocks quickly with his new club, hitting eight goals in his first 12 games.

Gilardino finished joint-top scorer in Italy's triumphant U-21 European Championship campaign in Germany. The same venue could see him achieve even greater heights with the senior side in 2006.

ITALY

STAR PLAYER

Luca Toni
D.O.B. 26 May 1977

Francesco Totti and Alessandro del Piero will be familiar names to many fans; Luca Toni may not register – yet – even though he will turn 28 just before the action gets under way in Germany. But the Fiorentina ace has been in such terrific form over the past two seasons that he looks likely to supplant del Piero in the Azzurri pecking order. Marcello Lippi may well favour a Toni-Gilardino strike partnership, which could provide the goals to erase the nightmare of Japan and Korea and Euro 2004.

Toni has served a long apprenticeship, his professional career dating back to 1994, when he joined Modena. He has been something of a butterfly since, turning out for eight clubs in the last decade. He got his Serie A opportunity with Vicenza in 2000, then had a spell with another top-flight side Brescia, playing alongside former golden boy Roberto Baggio, then winding down his career.

He stepped back down to Serie B with Palermo in 2003, but it proved a shrewd move as his 30 goals fired the club to promotion, and earned him a call-up to the national side. Toni bagged 20 more for Palermo in 2004–05, which persuaded Fiorentina to shell out £7 million last summer.

This season could scarcely have gone better for Toni. It kicked off with a hat-trick in Italy's 4–1 in Belarus in a World Cup qualifier. He then averaged a goal a game in his first 20 outings for Fiorentina, and two-thirds into the season he had done much to lift his team to fourth in the table, vying with the two Milan giants for second spot behind runaway leaders Juventus.

Fans of Fiorentina, who suffered demotion to Serie C after being declared bankrupt in 2002, must be pinching themselves at the speed of the club's resurgence. Yet success – particularly involving strikers – inevitably brings predators circling, and Barcelona are said to be interested in taking Toni to the Nou Camp this summer.

GHANA FIFA ranking: 48 • World Cup history: First appearance

Record-breakers in World Cup debut

Ghana has appeared in the African Nations Cup final a record seven times, and its four victories in the competition has been matched only by Egypt and Cameroon. Yet the Black Stars have had to sit and watch numerous African sides make their World Cup debut – until now.

Ghana hoped that its 1965 African Nations Cup win would have earned automatic qualification for the following year's finals in England, but on that occasion FIFA refused the African Football Federation's request. Forty years on, Ghana booked one of the five places up for grabs for Germany 2006 with a late flourish of four successive wins, having begun the campaign with a defeat at the hands of Burkina Faso.

The group from which Ghana emerged was not one of the strongest. South Africa, who host the 2010 finals, was a shadow of the side that made it to France '98 and Japan and Korea 2002. But that shouldn't detract from the achievement of a team steered through the latter stages of the qualifiers by veteran Serbian coach Radomir Dujkovic. He took over the reins in December 2004, having led Rwanda to the African Nations Cup finals earlier in the year. Chelsea's Michael Essien and Sammy Kuffour of Roma are the team's star names, yet Dujkovic's management style puts teamwork above individual virtuosity. He had no hesitation in dropping Kuffour from the squad over a disagreement, even when qualification remained in the balance.

STAR PLAYER
Michael Essien
D.O.B. 3 December 1982

Chelsea's pursuit of Michael Essien in the summer of 2005 was one of the longest-running transfer sagas of the close season. The midfielder threatened to go on strike if Lyon did not allow him to move to Stamford Bridge, and in the end Gerard Houllier, the boss of the French champions, bowed to the inevitable; Jose Mourinho got his man, at a cost of £24 million.

The powerful, combative Essien starred for Ghana in the World U-17 Championship in 1999. The following year he moved from Ghanaian side Liberty Professionals to Bastia, with whom he reached France's domestic cup final in 2002. He made his debut for the senior national team that year, helping Ghana reach the quarter-final of the African Nations Cup.

By the summer of 2003, Essien was a target of several big clubs, reigning champions Lyon eventually getting his signature. Essien helped Lyon win two more championships, establishing himself as one of Europe's top midfielders. Although regarded primarily as a defensive anchor, Essien hit five goals in 10 Champions League matches during Lyon's 2004–05 campaign. He did miss from the spot in the quarter-final shoot-out defeat by PSV, but his form that season earned him the country's Player of the Year award.

PATH TO THE FINALS:

WINNER IN AFRICA GROUP 2

	P	W	D	L	F	A	PTS
GHANA	10	6	3	1	17	4	21
CONGO	10	4	4	2	14	10	16
SOUTH AFRICA	10	5	1	4	12	14	16
BURKINA FASO	10	4	1	5	14	13	13
CAPE VERDE	10	3	1	6	8	15	10
UGANDA	10	2	2	6	6	15	8

UNITED STATES FIFA ranking: 6 • World Cup history: 8th appearance

Arena targets quarter-final spot

Although the United States reached the last four in the inaugural World Cup 76 years ago, and famously beat England in the 1950 tournament, it is the last 20 years which has seen the country rise to become a significant power in world football. Germany will mark the USA's fifth consecutive appearance in the finals, and Bruce Arena will be hoping his team can at least match the exploits of the 2002 squad, which reached the quarter-finals. That run saw the US qualify from a group at Portugal and Poland's expense, then put out arch-rivals Mexico before going down to Germany in somewhat unfortunate circumstances. It may have been a disappointment, but it helped bolster their FIFA ranking: when Arena's side pipped Mexico for top spot in the CONCACAF qualifying group, it stood at eight in the world table – one place ahead of England.

The USA narrowly missed out on being seeded for Germany; along with Holland, the team had just one ranking point fewer than Argentina and Italy. The vagaries of FIFA's system helped, but even so, the US is a side no opponents can afford to take lightly.

By the end of the qualifiers, the USA had won 38 of the 50 matches played since Japan and Korea, keeping 28 clean sheets. Ed Johnson and Landon Donovan, each with seven goals, were the team's main hitmen en route to Germany, with Brian McBride and DaMarcus Beasley weighing in with four apiece.

Teenage sensation Freddy Adu played no part in the qualifiers – he was only called into the senior squad for the first time in January – but the DC United attacking midfielder, who will turn 17 as the tournament gets under way, could force his way into the reckoning. Having played for the USA only at junior level, FIFA rules allow the Ghanaian-born prodigy to switch his allegiance. Ghana coach Ratomir Dujkovic will be watching with interest.

More certain of his place is evergreen 'keeper Kasey Keller, currently with Borussia Moenchengladbach, who passed the eight-hour mark without conceding when the team clinched its World Cup place with a 2–0 home win over Mexico. Steve Ralston and Beasley were the men on target. In front of Keller the imposing figure of giant defender Oguchi Onyewu presents a formidable obstacle to any opposition striker. Skipper Claudio Reyna has had an injury-hit season at Manchester City. Arena will be hoping his influential midfielder will be firing on all cylinders when the USA get down to business against Italy, the Czech Republic and Ghana, though even if the squad is fully fit, the two European big-hitters will be favourites to progress.

UNITED STATES

STAR PLAYER
Brian McBride
D.O.B. 19 June 1972

Brian McBride made his name with Major League Soccer side Columbus Crew. By 2000 he had been an international for seven years, and had the honour of scoring the USA's only goal at France '98, in the 2–1 defeat against Iran. But he had long harboured an ambition to play in England. David Moyes handed him the opportunity in September of that year, McBride moving to Deepdale on a season's loan. He had barely pulled on a Preston shirt when he took a knock to the arm which developed a clot and required surgery. It kept him out of action for months, yet he impressed enough to prompt Moyes to try and make the move permanent. The £1.75 million offer fell well short of Columbus' valuation and McBride returned to his MLS club.

McBride starred in Japan and Korea, hitting the back of the net against Mexico and Portugal to become the first American to score in two World Cup tournaments. His aerial power, ability to hold the ball up and strength off either foot brought Moyes knocking again, this time on behalf of Everton. He scored four goals in eight games, but competition at Goodison meant McBride was rarely a first choice starter, and by 2004 Everton were ready to listen to offers. Blackburn were interested, but Fulham, who had just lost Louis Saha to Manchester United, beat Rovers to his signature in January 2004.

Opposite: Brian McBride (r) and Oguchi Onyenwu (c) celebrate their sixth goal in the World Cup qualifier against Panama.

PATH TO THE FINALS:

WINNER IN CONCACAF FINAL QUALIFYING GROUP

	P	W	D	L	F	A	PTS
USA	10	7	1	2	16	6	22
MEXICO	10	7	1	2	22	9	22
COSTA RICA	10	5	1	4	15	14	16
TRINIDAD & TOBAGO	10	4	1	5	10	15	13
GUATEMALA	10	3	2	5	16	18	11
PANAMA	10	0	2	8	4	21	2

Nedved return boosts Czechs

For a country with no World Cup pedigree, the Czech Republic will be seen as serious contenders to lift the trophy in Germany. Although the No. 2-ranked team in the world hasn't quite lived up to expectations following a spectacular tournament debut at Euro '96, where they reached the final, the Czechs have an array of gifted players who can destroy any opposition on their day.

Orchestrator-in-chief is Pavel Nedved of Juventus, a survivor from Euro '96 who in 2003 became only the second Czech player in history to win the European Footballer of the Year award. Nedved retired after the 2004 European Championship but returned to help the side clinch a place in the World Cup Finals. The Czechs needed a victory in their final group match, in Finland to leapfrog Romania and claim second spot and a play-off place. They won the match 3–0, making it an aggregate 35 goals for the campaign; only Portugal matched that firepower in the European zone. Jan Koller, one of the few strikers who would be able to look Peter Crouch in the eye, scored nine times, putting him second to Portugal's Pauleta in the European zone. Victories home and away over Norway in the play-off secured the Czech Republic's place in the finals.

Nedved's return to the fold is a big plus for the side. For two other 30-pluses, Vladimir Smicer and Karel Poborsky, Germany will provide the chance of a glorious swansong. Smicer, who scored the only goal of the game in Norway, joined Bordeaux after signing off for Liverpool with a brilliant strike in the 2005 Champions League final. Ex-Manchester United speed merchant Poborsky, sporting a rather less flamboyant hairstyle these days, has been in good form for Sparta Prague.

Reds' fans rarely saw the best of Smicer, and Milan Baros was even more of an enigma. The Anfield faithful would have been ecstatic had Baros matched his prodigious international record of 26 goals in 39 games at club level. Five of those came at Euro 2004, Baros's scintillating performances earning him the tournament's Golden Boot. The Aston Villa man created the opening for Borussia Dortmund midfielder Tomas Rosicky to score against Norway in Prague, the goal which sealed the team's place in the finals.

After the play-off victory game Norway coach Aage Hareide was left shaking his head at a couple of wonder saves from 'keeper Petr Cech. Simply having Chelsea's shut-out king between the posts gives the Czech Republic a head start over most teams who will contest the finals.

On paper, Group E is the strongest of all, featuring three of the world's top 12 sides when the draw was made. It looks to be perm any two from the Czechs, Italy and the USA, with Ghana the probable whipping boys.

PATH TO THE FINALS:

RUNNER-UP EUROPE GROUP 1

	P	W	D	L	F	A	PTS
NETHERLANDS	12	10	2	0	27	3	32
CZECH REPUBLIC	12	9	0	3	35	12	27
ROMANIA	12	8	1	3	20	10	25
FINLAND	12	5	1	6	21	19	16
MACEDONIA	12	2	3	7	11	24	9
ARMENIA	12	1	1	10	3	25	4
ANDORRA	12	1	1	10	6	28	4

Right: Czech Republic's captain Pavel Nedved celebrates with teammate Vladimir Smicer after their qualification for the World Cup Finals.

CZECH REPUBLIC

STAR PLAYER

Petr Cech

D.O.B. 20 May 1982

Arguably the top goalkeeper in the world, Petr Cech exudes the same aura of cool invincibility that Peter Schmeichel once displayed for Manchester United and Denmark. In his debut season for the Blues, Cech passed the 1000-minute mark without having to pick the ball out of the net, beating Schmeichel's Premiership record. He conceded just 15 goals in Premiership matches, eclipsing the record of another illustrious name from the goalkeeping fraternity, David Seaman, whose Arsenal side shipped 17 in 1998–99. It was just the latest record-breaking chapter in the career of the six-foot-five colossus. In his Sparta Prague days Cech once went 15 hours without conceding, setting a new mark for the Czech league.

It was at Sparta, whom he joined in 2001, where Cech came to prominence. After just one season he moved to Rennes for £3.3 million, seven times the amount Sparta had paid to acquire his services. The French side didn't challenge for honours in his two seasons at the club, though Cech's personal stock continued to rise. He made his international debut in 2002, and was instrumental in the Czech Republic's victory in the European U-21 Championship that year. He kept a clean sheet against France in the final, and saved twice in the shoot-out.

Four clean sheets in eight Euro 2004 qualifiers took the Czech Republic to Portugal as group winners, relegating the Dutch masters to the play-offs. When the tournament got under way, Chelsea fans had the opportunity to see their latest acquisition in action, the £7 million deal to take Cech to the Bridge having already been done. They saw a man in sparkling form as he helped the Czechs reach the semis, where they went down to the tournament's surprise star turn, Greece. Cech had the consolation of being named in UEFA's squad of the tournament.

Group F

Brazil

Croatia

Australia

Japan

Monday June 12 Kaiserslautern
Australia v Japan

Tuesday June 13 Berlin
Brazil v Croatia

Sunday June 18 Munich and Nuremberg
Brazil v Australia, Japan v Croatia

Thursday June 22 Dortmund and Stuttgart
Japan v Brazil, Croatia v Australia

BRAZIL FIFA ranking: 1 • World Cup history: Record 18th appearance

Favourites looking for sixth win

Brazil are the only country to have contested every World Cup final, a proud record dating back to the inaugural tournament in 1930. The five-time winners and reigning champions go to Germany in their customary role as favourites, with a mountain of evidence to support the bookmakers' odds.

Carlos Alberto Parreira's side enters the fray as South American group winners, something Big Phil Scolari's men didn't manage four years ago. There were two reverses along the way, though in the powerful 10-country CONMEBOL zone, that represents an impressive campaign. One of those came in Ecuador, where all visiting teams had to face a 12th man – the altitude – and none left with three points. The other defeat was in the away fixture against old enemy Argentina, though Brazil did reverse that 3–1 scoreline when the teams met in Belo Horizonte.

That match was noteworthy for the four penalty kicks converted by Ronaldo. Only three counted – one had to be retaken because of encroachment – but it showed that the Japan and Korea Golden Boot winner is still one of the most clinical finishers in the business. Ronaldo wreaked havoc in the Argentina defence, winning each of the penalties himself. He was upended by Gabriel Heinze and Javier Mascherano for the first two, then completed his hat-trick in injury time after a mistimed challenge by Argentine 'keeper Pablo Cavallero.

That result, in June 2004, put Brazil top of the group, but a year later it was Argentina who held the advantage when it came to the final round. A 3–0 home win over Venezuela allowed Brazil to bridge the three-point deficit as Argentina slipped up in Uruguay. Brazil took top spot on goal difference.

Brazil laid down another marker to every other World Cup aspirant by winning last summer's Confederations Cup, which was also staged in Germany. They made a slow start, losing 1–0 to Mexico and dropping two points against Japan in the group phase. But in the latter stages the Brazilians slipped into overdrive. It was Germany in the semis, a repeat of the 2002 World Cup final. Two goals from man-of-the-match Adriano helped Brazil to a 3–2 victory, setting up yet another juicy encounter with Argentina in the final. In that match, Brazil turned on the style in a thumping 4–1 victory. Adriano grabbed another brace – making him the tournament's top scorer – with Kaka and Ronaldinho also getting on the scoresheet as Brazil added to their success in the inaugural Confederations Cup competition of 1997.

BRAZIL   Winners: 1958, 1962, 1970, 1994, 2002

A mix of youth and experience

Any team looking to topple Brazil has to contend with the fact that most of the 2002 vintage are still there: Cafu, Roberto Carlos, Lucio, Roque Junior, Gilberto Silva, Kleberson, plus, of course, Ronaldo and Ronaldinho. The main loss from that era is Rivaldo, but the stars who have emerged in the past four years more than compensate for his absence. There's Robinho and Julio Baptiste, the duo whose arrival at Real Madrid last summer rendered Michael Owen surplus to requirements; and in Adriano and Kaka, from the rival Milan clubs, Brazil have, respectively, a finisher to rival Ronaldo and an attacking midfielder as good as any in the world. The potential going forward is even greater than Japan and Korea, where Brazil hit 18 goals in their seven games en route to lifting the trophy.

If there is a weakness, it may be against teams who pose an aerial threat. And Brazil's legendary raiding full-backs are no spring chickens: Robert Carlos is 33, while Cafu will turn 36 during the tournament, although Madrid's new signing, right-back Cicinho looks promising. These may be minuscule crumbs of comfort, however, for this Brazil side has the firepower to accommodate the odd defensive blip.

Carlos Alberto Parreira, who led Brazil to victory at USA '94 with a less talented squad, says that his team won't simply rely on sexy football. 'I want to hear words like efficiency, productivity, winning well, sweat, perspiration and talent.' With their dazzling skills and a strong work ethic, Brazil look a good bet to win their second World Cup on European soil.

Right: Roberto Carlos (top) celebrates his goal against Venezuela with Kaka.

PATH TO THE FINALS:

WINNER IN SOUTH AMERICAN GROUP

	P	W	D	L	F	A	PTS
BRAZIL	18	9	7	2	35	17	34
ARGENTINA	18	10	4	4	29	17	34
ECUADOR	18	8	4	6	23	19	28
PARAGUAY	18	8	4	6	23	23	28
URUGUAY	18	6	7	5	23	28	25
COLOMBIA	18	6	6	6	24	16	24
CHILE	18	5	7	6	18	22	22
VENEZUELA	18	5	3	10	20	28	18
PERU	18	4	6	8	20	28	18
BOLIVIA	18	4	2	12	20	37	14

STAR PLAYER
Ronaldinho
D.O.B. 21 March 1980

When he burst onto the international scene, Ronaldo de Assis Moreira was dubbed Ronaldinho -'Little Ronaldo' – in deference to, and to distinguish him from, the team's premier striker. Ronaldo is still a fearsome striker, but since the last World Cup the younger man has eclipsed his international team-mate. Last autumn he picked up the European–World Footballer of the Year double, emulating Ronaldo's achievement of 1997 and 2002. He was a relative unknown to most fans in 2002; this time he goes into the tournament at the peak of his powers.

The man with the most famous buck-toothed smile in football joined Gremio at the age of seven. Like George Best, he was blessed with extraordinary natural gifts, and these he honed through tireless practice. He has probably the largest box of tricks in the game, a dazzling repertoire of skills, any one of which can bamboozle the best defender. Ashley Cole was on the receiving end of one of his party pieces in the Brazil v England quarter-final clash in Japan and Korea. In the surge from the halfway line which resulted in Rivaldo's equaliser he used 'the elastico', a move where he feints to go right by rolling his foot over the ball, then heads off in the opposite direction while the defender is still in the act of purchasing the dummy.

As well as making one goal that day, Ronaldinho scored the other. He insisted the free kick which sailed over David Seaman's head was premeditated. He was red carded that day, but had done enough to put Brazil into the semis.

Ronaldinho spent one more year at Paris St-Germain, the club he joined in 2001, but a mid-table French side was never going to provide him with a stage worthy of his skills. In his three years with Barcelona he has been key to the Catalan club's revival in fortunes. In 2004–05 Barca won their first La Liga title for six years, and by last Christmas were well on the way to making it back-to-back successes. Club coach Frank Rijkaard reportedly doesn't attempt to assign him a role or issue instructions; he simply invites Ronaldinho to go onto the field and do whatever comes naturally – which is usually devastatingly productive.

BRAZIL

STAR PLAYER

Kaka

D.O.B. 22 April 1982

Ricardo Izecson dos Santos Leite was given his footballing moniker by his younger brother, who couldn't get his tongue round the given name. Kaka made his debut for Brazil aged 19, just before the 2002 World Cup. He made a cameo appearance in the finals, but soaking up the big-tournament atmosphere was the main objective. This time round, many pundits are tipping the AC Milan man to be the star of the show, outshining Brazil's other first-choice attacking midfielder, a certain Ronaldinho.

AC Milan won the race for his signature in summer 2003, a number of European clubs having monitored the progress of a player who had earned rave reviews for his performances with Sao Paulo. Rivaldo had advised Milan of Kaka's ability, and, in an ironic twist, the latter's form meant the club could allow the veteran striker to leave the San Siro.

Kaka scored 10 goals in his debut season, contributing to Milan's first Serie A title for five years. His new club deployed him in a withdrawn role instead of out-and-out striker, and floating between midfield and attack makes him fiendishly difficult to pick up.

He enhanced his reputation in 2004–05, though Milan ceded the title to Juventus, and squandered a three-goal lead against Liverpool in the Champions League final. For his performances in Milan's run to the Istanbul showpiece, Kaka was named the tournament's best midfielder.

By the start of World Cup year Kaka had notched 12 goals in 36 appearances in a Brazil shirt, one of which came in the sparkling 4–1 win over Argentina in last summer's Confederations Cup final.

If he adds to his haul in Germany, fans will see one of the more unusual goal celebrations: he points his fingers to the sky as a sign of giving thanks to God, something he has done since he made a remarkable recovery from a diving-board accident which had threatened to end his career.

BRAZIL

STAR PLAYER

Ronaldo

D.O.B. 22 September 1976

'Ronaldo is still the player who makes the difference,' said coach Carlos Alberto Parreira, following the striker's hat-trick in the 3–1 home victory over Argentina in the qualifiers.

Ronaldo was a non-playing member of Brazil's victorious USA '94 squad, though at the next two tournaments he made a dramatic impact, for very different reasons. He went to France '98 as the reigning European and World Footballer of the Year. Just before the final, the 21-year-old was said to have suffered a seizure. He took the field, only to have a hugely disappointing game, and his performance set the tone for the entire team as they crashed 3–0 to the hosts.

Four years later, having recovered from a catalogue of injuries, Ronaldo set the record straight with a string of virtuoso displays. He won the Golden Boot, his haul including both goals in the final against Germany. England was the only opposition whose defence he failed to breach. It was no surprise that December, when Ronaldo picked up his third World Footballer of the Year award. That set a new record, though it was matched by Zidane a year later.

In the 12 years since Ronaldo left Cruzeiro to parade his skills on the European stage, PSV Eindhoven, Barcelona, Inter Milan and – since 2002 – Real Madrid, have all benefited from his explosive power, pace and unerring accuracy.

Ronaldo's 10 goals in the qualifiers was the best return in the South American zone. By the end of the campaign he had scored a phenomenal 56 goals in 88 games in his 11 years as an international. Should he find the net just once in Germany, he will set a new World Cup mark for his country; at the moment he has 12 to his name and is joint-record holder with the immortal Pele.

CROATIA FIFA ranking: 23 • World Cup history: 3rd appearance

Resurgence under new coach

In 1998, just seven years after becoming an independent nation following the disintegration of Yugoslavia, Croatia enjoyed a terrific World Cup debut, ended by hosts France at the semi-final stage. Four years later, the golden generation of Boksic, Prosinecki, Suker and co. was ageing, and Croatia went home early after defeats by Mexico and Ecuador. At Euro 2004 Croatia was well off the pace set by France and England.

Former Rapid Vienna star Zlatko Kranjcar, who replaced Otto Baric as coach after Portugal, deserves much of the credit for Croatia's resurgence. He guided the team through a group full of banana skins: Bulgaria and Sweden – both semi-finalists at USA '94 – and Lothar Matthaus' Hungary.

Croatia completed their programme unbeaten, taking top spot by virtue of a double over Sweden. Shakhtar Donetsk midfielder Darijo Srna scored the only goal on each occasion, and a point in Hungary ensured that they could not be overhauled.

Croatia has a resilient defence, conceding just five goals in ten matches. If they can get their noses in front, the Croatians have the wherewithal to hold on to their advantage; their Achilles' heel may be if they fall behind and have to chase the game.

Croatia will fancy their chances of coming out on top in the mini round-robin with Australia and Japan, and going through to the second round with favourites Brazil.

STAR PLAYER

Dado Prso

D.O.B. 5 November 1974

Dado Prso had all but given up hope of making the grade with a big club when he impressed for lowly French side San Raphael in a friendly against Monaco. Jean Tigana signed him, but with Thierry Henry and David Trezeguet on Monaco's books, Prso had a long loan spell with second-division side AC Ajaccio. He returned in 1999, helping Monaco win the championship for only the second time in a decade.

Lyon took over as top dog domestically, but Monaco did enjoy a superb run to the Champions League final in 2003–04. That included a stunning 8–3 victory over Deportivo la Coruna, Prso celebrating his 29th birthday by netting four times in under 25 minutes to equal the competition's record.

Prso made his international debut in the Euro 2004 qualifiers, scoring in both legs of the play-off against Slovenia which took Croatia to Portugal. Although Croatia fell at the first hurdle, Prso had a good tournament, and Rangers were pleased to bring a proven goalscorer to Ibrox. His goals helped the team snatch the title from Celtic on the last day of the 2004–05 season.

The man dubbed 'The Croatian van Basten' intends to quit international football after the World Cup, so will want to bow out with a better showing than Croatia managed at Euro 2004.

PATH TO THE FINALS:

WINNER IN EUROPE GROUP 8

	P	W	D	L	F	A	PTS
CROATIA	10	7	3	0	21	5	24
SWEDEN	10	8	0	2	30	4	24
BULGARIA	10	4	3	3	17	17	15
HUNGARY	10	4	2	4	13	14	14
ICELAND	10	1	1	8	14	26	4
MALTA	10	0	3	7	4	28	3

JAPAN FIFA ranking: 18 • World Cup history: 3rd appearance

Zico to build on 2002 success

Japan coach Zico may not have to mastermind a win over the team he graced in the 1980s, Brazil, but he will have to get the better of Croatia and dark horses Australia if the country is to emulate its run to the knockout stage on home soil in 2002.

Japan cruised through its opening group phase with maximum points, albeit against Oman, India and Singapore. There were five more wins in the final eliminator, the team's only reverse being a 2–1 defeat in Iran. Zico's men avenged that result at home, though by that time these two sides were streets ahead of Bahrain and North Korea with qualification in the bag.

11 wins out of 12 wasn't enough to impress all the fans, though, and the general feeling is that Japan hasn't really built on the foundations laid by Philippe Troussier four years ago. There was a call for Zico's head, late goals against Oman and North Korea salvaging unimpressive victories and helping to earn him a reprieve. Even so, the Brazilian ace will be stepping down when the World Cup glory trail grinds to a halt.

The centre-back partnership of captain Tsuneyasu Miyamoto and Yuji Nakazawa is solid, while Shinji Ono – back in the J-League after an injury-blighted four-year spell with Feyenoord – is an accomplished midfielder. With Celtic's Shunsuke Nakamura, West Brom's Junichi Inamoto and the talismanic Hidetoshi Nakata also in the middle of the park, that is the team's strongest area. Less certain is whether main strikers Atsushi Yanagisawa and Naohiro Takahara will give Japan enough firepower to get them out of a group with three tough opponents.

STAR PLAYER
Hidetoshi Nakata
D.O.B. 22 January 1977

Hidetoshi Nakata has a cult following in Asia of Beckhamesque proportions. During his seven years in Serie A, hordes of Japanese journalists reported on every last detail of the midfielder's performances and lifestyle in an attempt to satisfy Japanese fans' unquenchable thirst for news of their hero.

Winner of the Asian Footballer of the Year award in 1997 and 1998, Nakata added an Italian championship to his cv in 2001, during his time with Roma. A year later he had a Coppa Italia winners' medal with Parma, his new club beating Juventus in the final. Last August he joined Bolton in a loan deal from Fiorentina, yet another shrewd piece of business on Sam Allardyce's part.

Nakata, who won his first cap in 1997 and featured in both of Japan's previous World Cup campaigns, is bullish about the team's chances in Germany. 'The age of a football match being decided solely on name and reputation has long gone. Nowadays things are getting much more even, and we don't fear anyone.'

PATH TO THE FINALS:

WINNER IN ASIA GROUP B

	P	W	D	L	F	A	PTS
JAPAN	6	5	0	1	9	4	15
IRAN	6	4	1	1	7	3	13
BAHRAIN	6	1	1	4	4	7	4
NORTH KOREA	6	1	0	5	5	11	3

Socceroos are the dark horses

Following the 2002 World Cup, the Oceania countries received assurances that the winner of their group would be awarded an automatic place in the 2006 finals. In the event, those pledges evaporated, and the group winners once again had to face the fifth-placed team in South America's section in a final eliminator. That pitted Australia against Uruguay, a repeat of the 2002 play-off. This time, however, the Socceroos came out on top. The tie went to a shoot-out, and after Middlesbrough 'keeper Mark Schwarzer saved twice, it was left to former Coventry and Portsmouth striker John Aloisi to score the goal which took Australia to a World Cup for only the second time in the country's history.

Australia's triumph was the latest example of the Midas touch from Dutch coach Guus Hiddink. The man who steered South Korea to the semi-finals in 2002 had taken the helm just four weeks earlier, combining the Socceroos job with his coaching role at PSV Eindhoven.

Unlike the part-timers of 1974 – for whom a point against Chile and a 3–0 defeat against eventual winners West Germany represented an honourable return – the class of 2006 includes a host of top players plying their trade in Europe. As well as a strong Premiership contingent, notably Mark Viduka, Harry Kewell, Tim Cahill and Blackburn Rovers pair Lucas Neill and Brett Emerton, the Socceroos also boast two Serie A stars in Marco Bresciano and Vince Grella, who both play for Parma.

Sven-Goran Eriksson named Australia as one of the teams he hoped to avoid in the draw, while Kewell tips his side to be the tournament's dark horses, citing Greece's shock victory at Euro 2004 as a precedent. The Liverpool midfielder warned that opponents would take Australia lightly at their peril. England certainly appeared guilty of that at Upton Park in 2003, when the Socceroos ran out 3–1 winners, albeit in a friendly where Eriksson rang a number of changes. That result, together with the win over Uruguay and victories over France and Brazil in recent years, means that Australia has taken the scalps of four former world champions. The Socceroos may not expect to beat favourites Brazil this time, but will fancy their chances against Croatia, while Japan may not be so formidable this time round without home advantage.

AUSTRALIA

STAR PLAYER

Tim Cahill

D.O.B. 6 December 1979

Everton boss David Moyes believes that in Tim Cahill he has an attacking midfielder to rival Frank Lampard. Cahill top-scored with 12 goals in 2004–05, following his £2 million move from Millwall. His form and goals during that campaign played a significant part in helping Everton to finish fourth in the Premiership, in a season when many pundits expected the team to struggle. Certainly, at less than a fifth of the amount Chelsea paid for Lampard in 2001, Cahill represented one of the bargains of the season.

Cahill played for his home-town club Sydney United as a youngster, and also turned out for Western Samoa in an U-20 international when he was just 14. That solitary appearance was to have repercussions as he moved up the ladder and set his sights on international football with Australia.

The midfielder joined Millwall in 1997, making more than 200 games for the club over the next seven years and notching over 50 goals. The most famous of those was the strike which beat Sunderland in the 2004 FA Cup semi-final. Millwall went down 3–0 to Manchester United at the Millennium Stadium showpiece, but for Cahill that disappointment was ameliorated by a 'dream move' to Everton.

He also made his long-awaited international debut that spring. Former coach Frank Farina was finally able to select Cahill following a relaxation in FIFA's eligibility rules, and he got his international career off to a fine start by helping Australia reach the quarter-final at the Athens Olympics. He continued his hot scoring streak at the top level, hitting six goals in his first seven games for the Socceroos. Cahill rounded off a memorable 12 months by being named Oceania's Player of the Year for 2004, ahead of team-mates Mark Schwarzer and Marco Bresciano.

A true box-to-box midfielder who loves to be in the thick of the action, Cahill combines uncompromising defending with an eye for goal. His late runs into the box will pose a problem for any defence, as will his tremendous aerial power.

PATH TO THE FINALS:

**WINNER IN OCEANIA GROUP
THEN WINNER OF PLAY-OFF AGAINST URUGUAY**

	P	W	D	L	F	A	PTS
AUSTRALIA	5	4	1	0	21	3	13
SOLOMON ISLANDS	5	3	1	1	9	6	10
NEW ZEALAND	5	3	0	2	17	5	9
FIJI	5	1	1	3	3	10	4
TAHITI	5	1	1	3	2	24	4
VANUATU	5	1	0	4	5	8	3

Group G

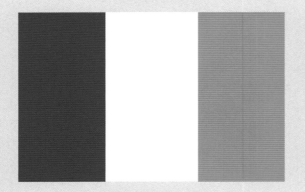

France

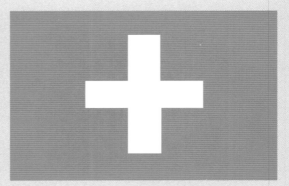

Switzerland

South Korea

Togo

Tuesday June 13 Stuttgart and Frankfurt
France v Switzerland, South Korea v Togo

Sunday June 18 Leipzig
France v South Korea

Monday June 19 Dortmund
Togo v Switzerland

Friday June 23 Cologne and Hanover
Togo v France, Switzerland v South Korea

FRANCE FIFA ranking: 5 World Cup history: 12th appearance

Last hurrah for Zidane and co.?

The 1998 World Cup winners topped a desperately tight qualifying group which evolved into a tense four-way scrap. A piece of Thierry Henry magic gave France a 1–0 away win against the Republic of Ireland, which turned out to be the only positive result involving the four contenders; every other game involving those two countries, plus Switzerland and Israel, was drawn.

It was hardly an emphatic campaign against opposition Les Bleus might have been expected to brush aside more easily, yet France did emerge as one of only six countries to make it to Germany unbeaten. The team was certainly mean at the back, conceding just twice – in Israel and at home to Switzerland – but they hardly set the pulse racing in attack. France plundered just 10 goals from their first nine games, and even though they rounded off their programme with the flourish of a 4–0 home victory over Cyprus, 14 goals was still the lowest total registered by any of the 31 qualifiers – 53 less than that amassed by top scorers Mexico! For a squad that boasted the striking talents of Djibril Cisse and David Trezeguet, as well as the mercurial Henry, it was a puzzling statistic.

STAR PLAYER
Patrick Vieira
D.O.B. 23 June 1976

Patrick Vieira departed for Juventus last summer after almost a decade of glittering service at Highbury. Many initially thought £13.7 million for a 29-year-old midfielder represented good business. By Christmas, however, the fans – and even some of the players – were voicing their opinion that the gaping void left by the former captain was the single biggest reason for the Gunners' indifferent season by their high standards.

The Vieira family relocated to Paris when Patrick was a youngster. He made his debut for Cannes at the age of 17, and within two years he was made captain, the youngest skipper of a French top-flight side.

He struggled to get a first-team start during a brief spell at AC Milan, and in 1996 new Gunners coach Arsene Wenger resurrected Vieira's stalled career. He and compatriot Emmanuel Petit formed a formidable midfield axis which drove Arsenal to the double in 1998. He wasn't yet a regular for France, though he did come on as substitute in that year's World Cup final against Brazil, setting up Petit for the third goal in the 3–0 victory.

Vieira picked up a winners medal at Euro 2000, and a second double followed with Arsenal in 2001–02. He took over from Tony Adams as club captain, and in 2003–04 led the side to another Premiership title, Arsenal becoming the first top-flight side to complete its league programme unbeaten since Preston's 'Invincibles' in 1888–89.

Vieira signed off for Arsenal last summer by converting the penalty which brought The FA Cup to Highbury for the fourth time during his nine years at the club.

FRANCE Winners: 1998

Recreating the magic of '98

Coach Raymond Domenech is looking to the old guard to try and recreate the magic of eight years ago. Architect-in-chief Zinedine Zidane came out of retirement after France's lacklustre start to their qualifying series. Lilian Thuram and Claude Makelele followed suit, while in a friendly against Costa Rica last November Nicolas Anelka made his first appearance in over three years for Les Bleus, celebrating his return to international football with a goal. Fabien Barthez is still around, too, though these days there is no Laurent Blanc on hand to plant a good-luck kiss on the 'keeper's bald pate. Barthez remained the country's No. 1 choice until a spitting incident in 2005 brought a six-month ban. Lyon's Gregory Coupet took over between the sticks, and it is uncertain whether the 34-year-old former Manchester United man will regain his place.

Chelsea fans know all about William Gallas's credentials in defence, but Jean-Alain Boumsong will have to produce considerably better form than he has shown thus far for Newcastle United; the Toon Army have been less than enamoured with his displays since he joined the Magpies from Rangers last year. Whoever plays in central defence will, of course, have the luxury of being protected by two of the best enforcers in the business: Makelele and Patrick Vieira.

The same cry that went up in the qualifiers will no doubt again be heard when Group G gets under way in the finals: Surely France will be too strong for their opponents…. That opposition again includes Switzerland, who will go into their match in Stuttgart unbowed after sharing the spoils in the two qualifiers. Then there are minnows Togo; little is expected of the side ranked 59 in the world, although they did make it to Germany at the expense of Senegal – the team that inflicted a shock 1–0 defeat on France in the curtain-raiser four years ago. South Korea are unlikely to present the threat which carried them to the semis on home soil in 2002. France should thus ease into the knockout phase, although the same was said before the team's shock first-round exit in Japan and Korea, when they were holders. Undoubtedly, there is an abundance of class in the squad, though this may prove a tournament too far for Zizou and co.

STAR PLAYER

Claude Makelele
D.O.B. 18 February 1973

There is a widely-held view that Real Madrid's lean spell in the past three years has much to do with the decision to sell midfield anchor Claude Makelele to Chelsea for £17 million in the summer of 2003. In his three years as a Galactico, Makelele helped Real win two Primera Liga titles, and the Champions League. When he picked up his Premiership winners medal with Chelsea in 2005, it completed a hat-trick of national championships, for he also won France's Championnat with his first club, Nantes, in 1995.

Makelele missed out on both the World Cup victory of 1998 and the Euro 2000 success. For him international football is synonymous with disappointment, France going down to Greece in the last eight at Euro 2004, following hard on the heels of the Japan and Korea nightmare. He retired after Portugal, but a year later he made a dramatic return to the international fold, a decision which has undoubtedly boosted France's chances in Germany.

FRANCE

STAR PLAYER

Thierry Henry

D.O.B. 17 August 1977

Gunners fans will view the World Cup jamboree with a degree of trepidation, fearing that Thierry Henry's appearance in the shop window may precipitate their star player's exit from Highbury. At the turn of the year, when he had just passed Ian Wright's mark to become Arsenal's all-time record goalscorer, Henry was said to be top of Barcelona's shopping list. Gooners thus had extra reason to hope the team would recover from its poor start to the season and secure a Champions League spot, since qualifying for Europe's premier competition was seen as pivotal to the striker's future.

Arsene Wenger knew what he was getting when he paid Juventus £11 million for Henry in 1999, having given the young striker his first taste of professional football at Monaco. He converted Henry from flying winger to central striker, since when he has been a veritable goal machine.

Henry combines grace and style with deadly end product, his performances earning him a string of honours and accolades. He was Footballer of the Year in 2003 and 2004, losing out to Pavel Nedved and Andriy Shevchenko respectively for FIFA's world award in those years. He has been Arsenal's top marksman every year since he moved to Highbury, and is a two-time winner of Europe's Golden Boot.

Henry was on target three times at the 1998 World Cup, though he didn't feature in the final. Japan and Korea was a disaster, both personally and for the team, as Henry was red carded against Uruguay and France limped out at the first hurdle.

When France secured its place in the finals, Henry's record for Les Bleus stood at 31 goals in 75 games. That put him joint-second with David Trezeguet in France's all-time list, 10 behind the legendary Michel Platini.

PATH TO THE FINALS:

WINNER IN EUROPE GROUP 4

	P	W	D	L	F	A	PTS
FRANCE	10	5	5	0	14	2	20
SWITZERLAND	10	4	6	0	18	7	18
ISRAEL	10	4	6	0	15	10	18
REP OF IRELAND	10	4	5	1	12	5	17
CYPRUS	10	1	1	8	8	20	4
FAROE ISLANDS	10	0	1	9	4	27	1

FRANCE

STAR PLAYER

Zinedine Zidane

D.O.B. 23 June 1972

Zinedine Zidane has won FIFA's World Footballer of the Year award three times, a record he shares with his Real Madrid teammate Ronaldo. He is a supreme artist – his much-copied double dragback is a joy to watch – but the box of tricks is invariably used to good effect.

Zidane made his name with Bordeaux, with whom he reached the 1996 UEFA Cup final. Juventus snapped him up for £3 million that year, and his flair and creativity brought the club successive Serie A titles. In 2001, a year after helping France to add the European Championship to their world crown, Zidane moved to the Bernabeu for a record £48 million. He was at his mesmerising best in the 2002 Champions League final, his stunning volley giving Real a 2–1 victory over Bayer Leverkusen.

Zidane scored twice with his head in the 1998 World Cup final victory over Brazil, but four years later he was carrying an injury and made only a fleeting contribution as France's attempt to retain the trophy ended in a whimper. 12 years after winning his first cap, 'Zizou' has said that Germany will be his international swansong.

SWITZERLAND FIFA ranking: 37 • World Cup history: 8th appearance

Contesting second spot

In a tight group chock full of draws, France's away win against the Republic of Ireland was the only positive result in the games involving the top four sides. Switzerland and Israel had identical records, but the former took the runner-up spot on the goal difference tie-breaker. The Swiss clinched a play-off place with a goalless draw in Dublin in their final match, a result which ended Ireland's hopes and ultimately cost Brian Kerr his job.

Switzerland was the only one of the three unseeded play-off sides in the Euro zone to cause an upset. While Slovakia and Norway fell, to Spain and the Czech Republic respectively, Switzerland ran out surprise winners over Turkey – semi-finalists in Japan and Korea and 11th in the world rankings, the highest rated team to miss out on the finals. Arsenal's Philippe Senderos was on target in the 2–0 home win, and the Swiss squeezed through on away goals after a volatile encounter in Istanbul. Alex Frei scored from the spot early on, and Marco Streller struck in the 84th minute; the Swiss went down 4–2 but it was enough to clinch their eighth trip to a World Cup.

Switzerland was again drawn with France, the team it shared the honours with in its group encounters – two goalless draws. France has brought some big guns out of retirement, though, so Switzerland will probably contest second spot with Japan, both sides being too strong for debutants Togo.

STAR PLAYER

Alex Frei

D.O.B. 15 July 1979

Alex Frei was a multi-talented youngster who was in his late teens before he decided on a career in professional football. He began his career at FC Basel, and also had a spell with the Geneva-based club Servette FC. He left to join French top-flight side Rennes in January 2003, and initially had something of a torrid time. He struggled to gain a regular first-team place, and was vilified for a spitting incident involving Steven Gerrard at Euro 2004, a misdemeanour which earned him a suspension.

Things have gone much better for the talented striker in the past 18 months. The turning point came when he put four goals past Fabien Barthez in a match against Marseille, and he won over the Rennes fans completely by scoring 20 goals in 2004–05. The new Championnat hotshot won Switzerland's Footballer of the Year award on the back of that performance.

Dubbed 'Petit Suisse' by Rennes supporters, Frei netted 16 goals in his first 32 games for Switzerland. He is not particularly tall or quick, but his clever runs and ability to find space have won him many admirers.

PATH TO THE FINALS:

RUNNER-UP IN EUROPE GROUP 4

	P	W	D	L	F	A	PTS
FRANCE	10	5	5	0	14	2	20
SWITZERLAND	10	4	6	0	18	7	18
ISRAEL	10	4	6	0	15	10	18
REP OF IRELAND	10	4	5	1	12	5	17
CYPRUS	10	1	1	8	8	20	4
FAROE ISLANDS	10	0	1	9	4	27	1

SOUTH KOREA FIFA ranking: 31 • World Cup history: 7th appearance

Can Advocaat repeat Hiddink trick?

No home advantage this time, so the task facing South Korea's Dutch coach, Dick Advocaat, is much stiffer than that of compatriot Guus Hiddink in 2002.

The team dropped four points in the first group phase, against lesser lights Lebanon, Vietnam and the Maldives, and was then beaten home and away by Saudi Arabia. Uzbekistan also held South Korea to a draw in the final group stage. A somewhat lacklustre campaign prompted the Korean FA to look for fresh inspiration at the helm, and the former Celtic boss was appointed.

Watch out for Lee Dong-gook – the man they call the 'Lion King' – who scored some of his trademark spectacular goals in the qualifiers. Pin-up boy Ahn Jung-hwan, whose golden goal dumped Italy out in the second round at the last World Cup, is still around. Manchester United's Park Ji-sung drives the midfield with Spurs' Lee Young-pyo, while Wolves fans can cheer on winger Seol Ki Hyeon. Korea's strength is going forward; Advocaat's problem is that the team has lost some experienced defenders over the last four years and will struggle against the world's elite strikers.

The saving grace for the surprise 2002 semi-finalists may be that Euro zone play-off winners Switzerland and outsiders Togo are also in Group G, so a place in the last 16 alongside favourites France is wide open.

STAR PLAYER

Park Ji-sung
D.O.B. 25 February 1981

Park Ji-sung and Lee Young-pyo became the first Koreans to grace the Premiership when they left PSV Eindhoven for Machester United and Tottenham respectively last summer. Roy Keane's departure and Paul Scholes' long-term injury made 'Ji' a vital cog in the United machine in a season when Smith, O'Shea and Ferdinand were all pressed into midfield service. £4 million looks a bargain price for a player who has adapted well to the rigours of Premiership football.

Park's performances in South Korea's run to the semis in 2002 earned him a move from Kyoto Purple Sanga to PSV. He was a bit-player at first, his outings restricted in PSV's 2002–03 championship success. After ceding the title to Ajax, PSV won the double in 2004–05, and this time Park was an integral member of Guus Hiddink's side. He turned in some top performances in PSV's terrific Champions League run, which was somewhat unluckily ended by AC Milan at the semi-final stage. Park scored in the 3–1 victory in the home leg, but it wasn't enough to stop Milan going through on away goals.

Skilful, quick and with boundless energy, Park has already passed the 50-cap mark at the age of 25 and is widely tipped to reach his century, emulating the achievement of legendary defender Hong Myung-Bo.

PATH TO THE FINALS:

RUNNER-UP IN ASIA GROUP A

	P	W	D	L	F	A	PTS
SAUDI ARABIA	6	4	2	0	10	1	14
SOUTH KOREA	6	3	1	2	9	5	10
UZBEKISTAN	6	1	2	3	7	11	5
KUWAIT	6	1	1	4	4	13	4

TOGO FIFA ranking: 59 • World Cup history: First appearance

The team that rocked Senegal

Togo's route to World Cup glory got off to an inauspicious start, with a defeat to lowly Equatorial Guinea in a pre-qualifier. Although they turned that tie around to reach the group stage proper, the Togolese lost their opening match to Zambia and came close to dropping out of the top 100 in the FIFA rankings. But Togo then went on a terrific unbeaten run, culminating in the win in Congo that secured its place in Germany.

Going into the biggest game in the country's history, Togo knew that defeat would leave the door open to Senegal, the 2002 quarter-finalists. Senegal beat Mali 3–0, but Togo came from behind to win their match, and El-Hadji Diouf and co. were out.

Seven wins and just one defeat represented a fine showing for a country with such a poor footballing pedigree. Much credit went to coach Stephen Keshi, who captained Nigeria at USA '94. Under his guidance the team shot up to 59 in the world, though of the finalists only Angola is ranked lower. Three defeats and an ignominious early exit at the African Cup of Nations in January gave an indication of the size of the task – and also cost Keshi his job.

Switzerland are not the strongest European opposition, but France and 2002 semi-finalists South Korea should prevent Togo's dream from extending beyond the group stage.

STAR PLAYER

Emmanuel Adebayor

D.O.B. 26 February 1984

Many 'Gooners' would have tuned in to this year's African Cup of Nations to see Arsene Wenger's latest acquisition in action. Togo star Emmanuel Adebayor was signed from Monaco just before he departed for Egypt to join up with the national squad. It wasn't a happy experience, Adebayor making the news mainly for a very public spat with the coach.

Even so, Arsenal look to have bought well. The tall, rangy Adebayor scored 11 goals in the qualifiers, making him the Africa zone's sharpest shooter. He was on target both home and away against Senegal, the four points taken from the group favourites proving crucial to Togo's World Cup bid. His performances earned him his country's Footballer of the Year award for 2004.

Many top clubs were said to be tracking Adebayor's progress, though some may have been deterred by his reputation for being abrasive. He fell out with Monaco, and also left his previous club, Metz, under a cloud. He made his debut for Metz at 17, but came to prominence when he scored 7 goals in 17 matches to help propel Didier Deschamps' Monaco to the 2004 Champions League final.

Adebayor has been likened to Kanu, his footballing hero, and when he signed for Arsenal he opted to take the number 25 shirt in honour of the former Gunner.

PATH TO THE FINALS:

WINNER IN AFRICA GROUP 1

	P	W	D	L	F	A	PTS
TOGO	10	7	2	1	20	8	23
SENEGAL	10	6	3	1	21	8	21
ZAMBIA	10	6	1	3	16	10	19
CONGO-BRAZZAVILLE	10	3	1	6	10	14	10
MALI	10	2	2	6	11	11	8
LIBERIA	10	1	1	8	3	27	4

Group H

Spain

Ukraine

Tunisia

Saudi Arabia

Wednesday June 14 Leipzig and Munich
Spain v Ukraine, Tunisia v Saudi Arabia

Monday June 19 Stuttgart and Hamburg
Spain v Tunisia, Saudi Arabia v Ukraine

Friday June 23 Kaiserslautern and Berlin
Saudi Arabia v Spain, Ukraine v Tunisia

Time to lose 'underachievers' tag

A sole European Championship victory at a time when the Beatles ruled the airwaves is scant return for the quality Spain has produced over the years. While Primera Liga sides full of native talent have won 15 European trophies since that 1964 success, the national team has merely consolidated its reputation for underachievement.

Reaching the finals hasn't been a problem: 2006 will be Spain's eighth successive World Cup, including 1982, when they hosted the jamboree. And in three of the past five tournaments the Spanish side has made it to the last eight, the shoot-out lottery costing them a place in the semis in both 1986 and 2002.

One of the survivors of the agonising defeat last time round – when Spain had two goals disallowed against co-hosts South Korea – is captain and talisman Raul. The legendary striker, idol of the Bernabeu with over 50 Champions League goals to his name since he made his Real Madrid debut as a 17-year-old over a decade ago, offered no excuses as his men were consigned to the play-offs. A draw in Lithuania, along with two more dropped points at home to Bosnia-Herzegovina, left Spain needing to beat Slovakia, who had edged Russia for the runner-up spot in Group 3. It was shades of Euro 2004, when Spain also came through a nervy play-off against Norway to qualify for Portugal. In the home leg against Slovakia Luis Garcia hit a hat-trick, while his Anfield teammate Fernando Morientes came off the bench to head the fifth in a 5–1 rout, the latter's goal putting him level in the all-time list with Emilio Butragueno – 'The Vulture' of Real Madrid's 1980s side.

That result made the visit to Bratislava little more than a sightseeing trip; it also showed that at their mercurial best Spain have the armoury to threaten any opposition. As well as the Liverpool contingent, the squad boasts Chelsea's del Horno and Arsenal's Reyes, plus the likes of Casillas, Puyol, Baraja and Xavi. And Germany may well be the place where 22-year-old Atletico Madrid striker Fernando Torres becomes a global star.

The knockout stage should be the very least expected of Luis Aragones's men; but then again, most thought the class of '98 would have come through a group including Nigeria, Paraguay and Bulgaria. A 6–1 thrashing of Bulgaria in the final game wasn't enough to prevent them falling at the first hurdle in France eight years ago. This time round they have to face Shevchenko and co. and a dangerous Tunisia side that went into the 2006 African Nations Cup as defending champions. Qualifying for the second phase is certainly no foregone conclusion for the team ranked sixth in world.

Above: Spanish players celebrate their second goal against Slovakia during their World Cup 2006 qualifying play-off first leg.

SPAIN

STAR PLAYER

Fernando Torres
D.O.B. 20 March 1984

Since making his tournament debut with three appearances at Euro 2004, Fernando Torres has established himself as one of the hottest properties on the Continent. Torres had just broken into the side when Spain went to Portugal. He didn't get on the scoresheet, the team hitting just two goals in a group which included the eventual finalists, Greece and the host nation.

Goals certainly are his business, though. Torres scored Spain's winner in the final of both the 2001 UEFA U-16 Championship and the 2002 U-19 Championship, picking up the golden boot in the latter tournament. He became Atletico Madrid's youngest ever scorer, after making his debut for the club he supported as a boy in 2000. Such prowess in one so young earned him the nickname 'El Nino' – the child. Torres hit 13 in 29 starts in 2002–03, his first full La Liga campaign, then the following season met the benchmark of all top strikers by scoring a goal every other game. He added a respectable 17 to his tally in 2004–05. At just 19 Torres was handed the captain's armband, a mark of his maturity as well as his influence on the pitch.

On the international front Torres found the net seven times in the qualifiers, six of those coming in a three-game blitz. He hit both goals in the 2–0 win in Belgium, plundered a hat-trick away to San Marino, and was also on target in the first leg of the play-off, when Spain thrashed Slovakia 5–1.

Jose Antonio Reyes, another star in Spain's pool of burgeoning young talent, is said to have urged Arsenal to wave their cheque-book in Madrid's direction. If Atletico decides to sell, no doubt a host of big clubs with deep pockets will form a not very orderly queue.

PATH TO THE FINALS:

RUNNER-UP IN EUROPE GROUP 7

	P	W	D	L	F	A	PTS
SERBIA & MONTENEGRO	10	6	4	0	16	1	22
SPAIN	10	5	5	0	19	3	20
BOSNIA-HERZEGOVINA	10	4	4	2	12	9	16
BELGIUM	10	3	3	4	16	11	12
LITHUANIA	10	2	4	4	8	9	10
SAN MARINO	10	0	0	10	2	40	0

UKRAINE FIFA ranking: 41 • World Cup history: First appearance

'Sheva' and Co. top tough group

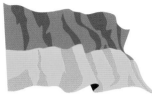

Following the disappointment of play-off defeats at the last two World Cups, Ukraine has reached its first major tournament. They did it the hard way, too, having to face European champions Greece, 2002 semi-finalists Turkey and a dangerous Denmark team. Ukraine went five points clear at the top of the table after a stunning 3–0 victory in Turkey. That gave them three wins and two draws from their opening five games, and they never looked like relinquishing the lead thereafter.

Coach Oleg Blokhin masterminded the campaign. The former Dynamo Moscow star briefly stood down in a row over his dual role as politician and national team coach, but that was soon resolved. A draw in Georgia put Ukraine into the finals, rendering the subsequent home defeat against the Turks and failure to beat Albania academic.

Virtually the entire squad is Ukraine-based, with players from Dynamo Kyiv, Shakhtar Donetsk and Dnipro forming the backbone. Two exceptions are striker Andrey Voronin, who plays for Bayer Leverkusen, and the country's one world class star, Andriy Shevchenko.

Group H seeds Spain are erratic but should go through, leaving the Ukraine vying for second spot with 2004 African Cup of Nations winners Tunisia.

STAR PLAYER
Andriy Shevchenko
D.O.B. 29 September 1976

In extra-time of the 2005 Champions League final, AC Milan fans were stunned as Jerzy Dudek pulled off an extraordinary double save from their top striker, Andriy Shevchenko. In the shoot-out it was his penalty miss that handed the crown to Liverpool. By Shevchenko's remarkable standards, it had been a bad day at the office, but he remains a veritable goal machine. 'Sheva' top-scored for Ukraine in the qualifiers with six goals; that put him on 28 in 63 international appearances.

Shevchenko made his name at Dynamo Kyiv. In 1990 the 13-year-old hotshot played for a Kyiv boys team which won a tournament staged in Wales. He was named best player, and presented with a pair of boots by Ian Rush.

Shevchenko won five successive Ukrainian championships with Dynamo, but it was his Champions League performances during that period which caught the eye, notably a hat-trick in a stunning 4–0 away win against Barcelona in 1997–98. The following season he topped the Champions League scoring chart as Kyiv beat Real Madrid in the quarter-final before going out to Bayern Munich.

Shevchenko plundered 24 goals in 1999–2000, his first term with AC Milan. That made him the league's top marksman, a feat he emulated in 2003–04, when he helped Milan to their first scudetto in five years. In December of that year he received the European Footballer of the Year award, emulating the achievement of former Kyiv star Igor Belanov in 1986.

PATH TO THE FINALS:

WINNER EUROPE GROUP 2

	P	W	D	L	F	A	PTS
UKRAINE	12	7	4	1	18	7	25
TURKEY	12	6	5	1	23	9	23
DENMARK	12	6	4	2	24	12	22
GREECE	12	6	3	3	15	9	21
ALBANIA	12	4	1	7	11	20	13
GEORGIA	12	2	4	6	14	25	10
KAZAKHSTAN	12	0	1	11	6	29	1

TUNISIA FIFA ranking: 23 • World Cup history: 4th appearance

Consecutive appearance for group winners

Tunisia will be looking to improve on its previous two showings: one draw at France '98, another in Japan and Korea, and group wooden spoonists on each occasion.

The 2004 African Cup of Nations champions won just one of their first four qualifiers, leaving arch-rivals Morocco in the box seat. A 7–0 trouncing of Malawi kick-started a run of five wins on, and it all came down to the home clash with Morocco in the final round. Unbeaten Morocco needed a win, Tunisia only had to avoid defeat. Morocco twice went ahead but Adel Chadli made it 2–2 and Tunisia was through.

Watch out for Brazilian-born striker Francileudo dos Santos, who hit six goals during the qualifiers. Veteran captain Riadh Bouazizi is the driving force in midfield, while Paris Saint-Germain's Slim Benachour is the playmaker, dubbed 'The Zidane of the Carthage Eagles'. But the key man is Roger Lemerre, who led France to victory at Euro 2000 and masterminded Tunisia's 2–1 victory in the final of the 2004 African Cup of Nations – over Morocco.

Lemerre has moulded a unit capable of repeating Tunisia's achievement of 1978, when a 3–1 win over Mexico made it the first African country to win a game at the finals. Saudi Arabia, ranked four places lower, will be the prime target for a second World Cup win in Germany, and a second-round appearance is a possibility for the only African side from Japan and Korea to reach these finals.

STAR PLAYER

Radhi Jaidi
D.O.B. 30 August 1975

How well the Tunisian defence stands up to the likes of Andriy Shevchenko, Fernando Torres and Raul could be the key to whether the country can progress beyond the group stage for the first time. The imposing figure of Radhi Jaidi, with over 80 caps to his name, will be the linchpin at the back as Tunisia try to carve out a result against the two European big guns in Group H.

For more than a decade Jaidi had been a stalwart for Esperance, Tunisia's perennial league champions, when he seized on the opportunity of a move to the Premiership in summer 2004. It was another nifty deal on Big Sam's part, Jaidi weighing in with a useful five goals in 28 appearances in his debut season. It wasn't quite the set-piece scoring rate he had been used to – a goal every two or three games had been the norm for Esperance – but the 6ft 4in defender has a nose for when and where to make his runs, and aerial power that his club manager enthuses over.

In the modern game, rugged defenders routinely accumulate cards, yet Jaidi prides himself on a fine disciplinary record, which he puts down to skill and timing.

PATH TO THE FINALS:

WINNER IN AFRICA GROUP 5

	P	W	D	L	F	A	PTS
TUNISIA	10	6	3	1	25	9	21
MOROCCO	10	5	5	0	17	7	20
GUINEA	10	5	2	3	15	10	17
KENYA	10	3	1	6	8	17	10
BOTSWANA	10	3	0	7	10	18	9
MALAWI	10	1	3	6	12	26	6

SAUDI ARABIA   FIFA ranking: 35 • World Cup history: 4th appearance

Four tournaments in a row

Saudi Arabia will be keen to put up a better show than it managed in Japan and Korea – and it could hardly be worse: three defeats, including an 8-0 mauling by Germany, and not a single goal scored. The team qualified comfortably enough, though with the standard of the opposition, an impressive record can be somewhat deceptive. Turkmenistan, Indonesia and Sri Lanka were the fall-guys as the Saudis scored maximum points in their preliminary group. They were up against Uzbekistan and Kuwait in the final round, though with South Korea also in there, the Saudi side did well to maintain its unbeaten record and ship just one goal. Saudi chalked up a double over the 2002 semi-finalists.

Legendary 'keeper Mohammed al-Deayea, who played in the last three tournaments and set a new world record with 173 caps, has gone, but in Mabrouk Zayed, who plays for Al-Ittihad, Saudi has unearthed another star between the sticks. In front of him is club teammate Hamad Al Montashari, the 2005 Asian Footballer of the Year, who marshals a tight defence. But the key man is still captain and superstar Sami al-Jaber, a survivor of Saudi's World Cup debut at USA '94, where the team finished ahead of Belgium and Morocco to reach the last 16. It may be four tournaments in a row, but faced with two strong European sides and the 2004 African Cup of Nations winners, Saudi Arabia look likely whipping boys again.

STAR PLAYER
Sami al-Jaber
D.O.B. 11 December 1972

Lack of top-level experience will inevitably hinder Saudi Arabia's chances, making the contribution of veteran captain Sami al-Jaber all the more crucial. His loan spell with Wolves in 2000 makes him one of the few players from the region to have played in Europe.

Having made his debut for Saudi at 17, al-Jaber has been an international for just about half his life. He scored on his debut, in 1990, and was also on target in the 2–1 win over Morocco at USA '94, Saudi Arabia's first World Cup victory and one of only two wins in 10 matches to date. He got on the scoresheet at France '98, too, becoming the first Asian footballer to hit the net in successive tournaments, though it didn't prevent the team from propping up the group.

Thirty-three-year-old al-Jaber came out of international retirement to help guide his country to the finals, scoring three goals along the way. Last autumn he passed the 150-cap mark, one of only six players to reach it. His influence on the younger members of the team will be just as crucial as his personal form if the three-time Asian champions are to stand any chance of repeating their 1994 heroics.

PATH TO THE FINALS:

RUNNER-UP IN ASIA GROUP A

	P	W	D	L	F	A	PTS
SAUDI ARABIA	6	4	2	0	10	1	14
SOUTH KOREA	6	3	1	2	9	5	10
UZBEKISTAN	6	1	2	3	7	11	5
KUWAIT	6	1	1	4	4	13	4

World Cup Venues

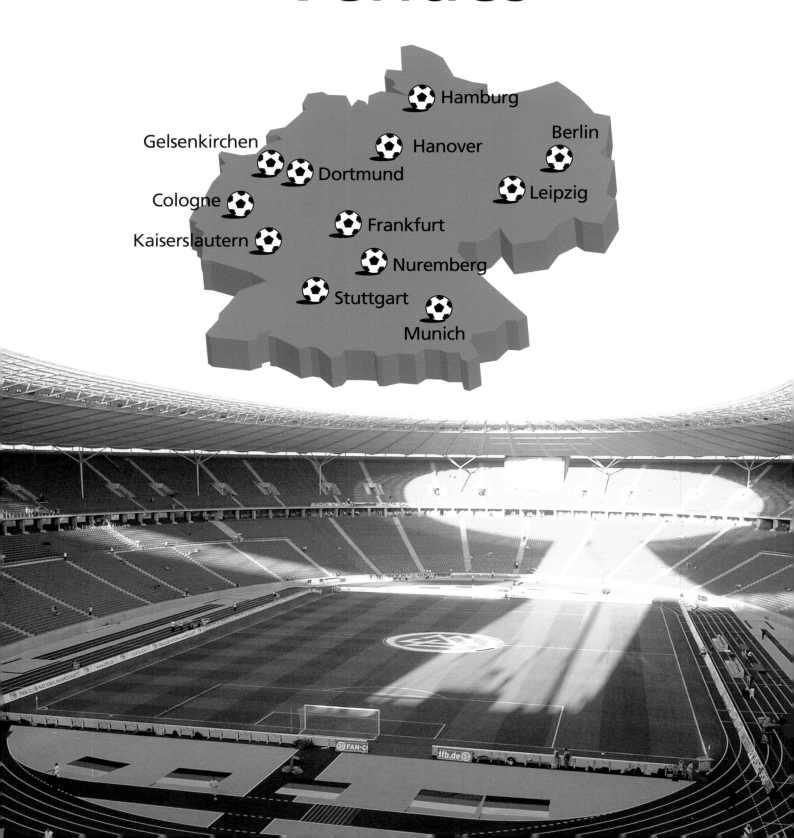

Hamburg

Gelsenkirchen

Berlin

Hanover

Dortmund

Leipzig

Cologne

Frankfurt

Kaiserslautern

Nuremberg

Stuttgart

Munich

Above: England will face Sweden in their final group match on 20 June in Cologne.
Opposite: Berlin's Olympiastadion was chosen as the venue for the World Cup Final on 9 July.

Berlin

The Berlin Olympic Stadium has hosted its fair share of momentous events, but 9 July 2006 is destined to eclipse everything that has gone before. A global audience of well over a billion is set to follow the 2006 FIFA World Cup Final live on TV. American sprinter Jesse Owens won four gold medals here at the 1936 Olympic Games. Today, one of the avenues leading to the ground and a VIP lounge bear the great runner's name. The stadium has staged the German Cup Final since 1985.

Cologne

The people of Cologne felt a mixture of relief and exhilaration when their new stadium finally opened in the spring of 2004: Germany's fourth-largest city failed to make the cut in 1974 and missed out on that year's FIFA World Cup. The new 46,000 capacity purpose-built football arena ensured Cologne won this time around against stiff competition from neighbouring cities.

Dortmund

Known nationwide as the Bundesliga's opera house, the Westfalenstadion was originally built for the 1974 FIFA World Cup. Borussia Dortmund play their home games here, usually in front of sell-out crowds. Some 25,000 of these fans roar on their beloved Borussia from the famous South Stand terraces, an awesome and fearful prospect for the visiting team. No fewer than 1.4 million spectators thronged to Germany's biggest stadium in 2004–05, making an average attendance of over 77,000 and a Bundesliga and European record.

BERLIN
STADIUM: OLYMPIASTADION
TOTAL SEATING CAPACITY: 66,021
GROUP STAGE: 56,358
QUARTER-FINALS: 56,316
FINAL: 55,562

COLOGNE
STADIUM: FIFA WORLD CUP STADIUM
TOTAL SEATING CAPACITY: 40,590
GROUP STAGE: 35,926
ROUND OF SIXTEEN: 35,580

DORTMUND
STADIUM: WESTFALENSTADION
TOTAL SEATING CAPACITY: 60,285
GROUP STAGE: 50,768
ROUND OF SIXTEEN: 50,276
SEMI-FINALS: 49,876

Frankfurt

A minimalist supporting structure combined with a flood of natural light through the translucent roof give the FIFA World Cup Stadium in Frankfurt a cathedral-like atmosphere. Work on the futuristic stadium began in 2002, resulting in a worthy successor to the 'old' Waldstadion and its plethora of sporting memories, including the waterlogged semi-final between Poland and West Germany in 1974, and the Muhammad Ali vs Karl Mildenberger bout in 1966. Most recently, the new stadium hosted the 2005 FIFA Confederations Cup Final between Brazil and Argentina.

Gelsenkirchen

The arena was officially opened on 13 and 14 August 2001, immediately setting a new benchmark in the art of stadium construction. European governing body UEFA assigned the multifunctional arena to the highest-possible five-star category, commenting: 'This venue more than fulfils the necessary criteria, and might even qualify as a "six-star stadium".'

'This stadium is a pilot project for the whole world', said FIFA President Joseph S. Blatter. The Champions League Final was staged here on 27 May 2004. The FIFA World Cup Stadium Gelsenkirchen project was financed by private capital.

Hamburg

The new stadium in Hamburg, inaugurated on 2 September 2000 with a match between Germany and Greece, boasts a capacity of 56,114 for Bundesliga matches. The arena officially qualifies as one of the best football grounds in Europe after earning a maximum five stars from UEFA.

Work on the new ground started in March 1998: the old Volksparkstadion was demolished in four stages, the pitch rotated and the stands rebuilt. The function rooms, VIP and media areas were completely remodelled. All the spectator areas are now covered. Electronic access controls featuring machine-readable microchip technology were introduced for the 2005–06 season. The stadium is home to Hamburg SV, the only club ever-present in the German top-flight throughout the Bundesliga's 42-year history.

FRANKFURT
STADIUM: WALDSTADION
TOTAL SEATING CAPACITY: 43,324
GROUP STAGE: 38,437
QUARTER-FINALS: 37,925

GELSENKIRCHEN
STADIUM: FIFA WORLD CUP STADIUM
TOTAL SEATING CAPACITY: 48,426
GROUP STAGE: 43,920
QUARTER-FINALS: 43,574

HAMBURG
STADIUM: FIFA WORLD CUP STADIUM
TOTAL SEATING CAPACITY: 45,442
GROUP STAGE: 40,918
QUARTER-FINALS: 40,226

Hanover

Hanover, capital city of the state of Lower Saxony, is ready to welcome visiting fans with its purpose-built football stadium. Work to reconstruct the Niedersachsenstadion was completed ahead of schedule in December 2004. The arena, boasting a 50,000 capacity for Bundesliga fixtures, features a free-standing, 2,500 tonne roof supporting structure. The sections of the roof overhanging the playing surface are constructed from an ultra-violet permeable foil, ensuring the pitch receives the light it needs to remain in perfect condition.

Leipzig

The completion of the Leipzig Zentralstadion in December 2003 gave the trading city of Leipzig an architecturally distinctive and technically advanced football stadium. The 45,000-seat arena was commissioned specifically for the 2006 FIFA World Cup. Following reunification, Leipzig is at the centre of a forward-looking, dynamic region in the east of the German Federal Republic. As one of a total of 12 FIFA World Cup host cities, Leipzig will stage four group stage matches and a match in the round of sixteen.

HANOVER
STADIUM: FIFA WORLD CUP STADIUM HANOVER
TOTAL SEATING CAPACITY: 39,297
GROUP STAGE: 34,311
ROUND OF SIXTEEN: 33,965

LEIPZIG
STADIUM: ZENTRALSTADION
TOTAL SEATING CAPACITY: 38,898
GROUP STAGE: 34,384
ROUND OF SIXTEEN: 34,038

Above: Frankfurt's Waldstadion, venue for England's opening game against Paraguay on 10 June.
Opposite: Dortmund will host the first of the semi-finals on 4 July.

Kaiserslautern

Situated on the Betzenberg, a 40 metre sandstone hillock at the heart of the Palatinate city, the Fritz-Walter-Stadion opened its doors in 1920 (although it was only named after the legendary West German 1954 World Cup-winning captain in 1985). Changing times and tastes are visible in the architecture at the purpose-built football arena, home to 1. FC Kaiserslautern. The ground has a distinctly modular feel because of a series of additions and extensions over the decades. Reconstruction for the FIFA World Cup was completed in November 2005. The final phase of the project comprised extensions to the West and South stands, and reconstruction of the North stand. A media tower and VIP tower will occupy the northern corners of the ground.

Munich

The stadium chosen to host the German national team in the opening match of the 2006 FIFA World Cup on 9 June 2006 boasts a truly unique exterior, guaranteeing the stadium a place among the most unusual and spectacular venues in the world. The smooth facade formed from translucent, lozenge-shaped cushions glows in a variety of colours to imbue the structure with a shimmering, magical poetry. The 66,000 capacity stadium was inaugurated on 30 and 31 May 2005 by joint owners TSV 1860 Munich and FC Bayern Munich, Germany's most successful club. The first Bundesliga goal at the new ground was scored by England international Owen Hargreaves in Bayern's 3–0 victory over Borussia Monchengladbach.

KAISERSLAUTERN
STADIUM: FRITZ-WALTER-STADION
TOTAL SEATING CAPACITY: 39,820
GROUP STAGE: 37,084
ROUND OF SIXTEEN: 36,392

MUNICH
STADIUM: ALLIANZ ARENA
TOTAL SEATING CAPACITY: 59,416
GROUP STAGE: 52,782
ROUND OF SIXTEEN: 52,636
SEMI-FINALS: 52,090

Above: England will face Trinidad & Tobago at the Franken-Stadion in Nuremberg on 15 June.
Opposite: The Allianz Arena in Munich which will host both the opening game and the second semi-final of the competition.

Nuremberg

Only three of the stadiums at the 2006 FIFA World Cup continue to feature an athletics track: Berlin, Stuttgart and Nuremberg. The remaining venues are all football-only stadiums. Nevertheless, the Franken-Stadion boasts a unique atmosphere and superb facilities.

Stuttgart

The citizens of Stuttgart have experienced sporting, cultural and even historic scenes at their Gottlieb-Daimler-Stadion. Germany met Switzerland here in 1950 in the first international on German soil following the end of the Second World War. Forty years later, on 19 December 1990, the stadium hosted the first international since reunification, another contest between the Germans and their Swiss neighbours. The ground has been the venue for the European Champions Cup Final, a concert by the Rolling Stones, FIFA World Cup and European Championship matches, and the athletics World Championships. Current Germany coach Jürgen Klinsmann made his final appearance as a player here on 24 May 1999.

NUREMBERG
STADIUM: FRANKEN-STADION
TOTAL SEATING CAPACITY: 36,898
GROUP STAGE: 32,341
ROUND OF SIXTEEN: 31,995

STUTTGART
STADIUM: GOTTLIEB-DAIMLER-STADION
TOTAL SEATING CAPACITY: 47,757
GROUP STAGE: 39,030
ROUND OF SIXTEEN: 38,884
THIRD PLACE MATCH: 38,538

The History of the World Cup

The formation of FIFA

The twin ideas of forming a body to regulate world football, and staging a global championship as the sport's flagship, were mooted in the early years of the twentieth century. The English FA took a lofty, insular approach to the scheme, and didn't attend the meeting in Paris in May 1904 where FIFA was established. The FA slowly thawed, but even then it insisted that entry to any proposed international tournament was optional; it didn't want to be bound to send a team to some far-flung corner of the planet.

The Olympic Games was somewhat quicker off the mark. Football became an official event in 1908, the fourth Games of the modern Olympiad, and for the next 20 years remained the only major international football tournament.

FIFA, meanwhile, found it no easy task to get its own long-cherished idea of a world championship off the ground. World War I intervened, and even when the conflict ended, the British Associations refused to play against the defeated countries: Austria, Hungary and Germany. They withdrew from FIFA in 1920, and even attempted to form a rival world body. New FIFA president Jules Rimet was a keen advocate of a global competition, but the dream still looked a far-distant prospect.

Soccer at the Olympics

In fact, it took another decade for the dream to be realised. As the ill feeling following WW1 receded, a new issue came to the fore which helped FIFA's cause: 'shamateurism'. In the 1920s professionalism was by no means universal throughout the footballing world – at least, not officially. The Olympic authorities circumvented the issue by endorsing 'broken-time' payments – allowing players to be recompensed for lost earnings – which in theory kept the ethos of amateurism intact. They did so reluctantly, under pressure from FIFA, but could scarcely have done otherwise. Football was a huge money-spinner for the Olympics. At the 1928 Games, staged in Amsterdam, football provided over one-third of the total revenue, and more than twice that of the next most popular sport, athletics.

However, broken-time payments were, in many cases, a complete sham. In Italy and Uruguay, for

Above: FIFA President Jules Rimet presents the World Cup to Dr Paul Jude, President of the Uruguayan Football Association, following his team's 4–2 win in the Final of the inaugural competition.
Opposite: Pele, who missed the final through injury, displays the Jules Rimet trophy in 1962.

example, players could be nominally on the books of an employer, when they were in fact full-time professionals with their clubs. The FA had faced this same issue 50 years earlier, eventually embracing professional football in 1885.

Uruguay host first finals

By the late 1920s, it was clear that the days of the Olympic Games as the world's premier football tournament were numbered. Countries could either enter de facto professional – and thus ineligible – players, or they could play to Olympic rules, and thus deny the tournament of the world's greatest exponents of the game. Both situations were equally unsatisfactory. Football was crying out for an unrestricted world championship, and at a FIFA meeting in 1929, the decision was taken to hold an international tournament within the next year. Uruguay, winners of the 1924 and 1928 Olympic titles, offered to stage the competition to mark the centenary of the country's independence. The World Cup was born.

It wasn't an easy birth, though. The prospect of a long sea trip to South America deterred many of Europe's top football-playing countries, despite the generous offer of the Uruguayan authorities to pay their expenses.

France, Belgium, Yugoslavia and Romania flew the flag for Europe; the other nine contenders were from the Americas. The British associations had once again seceded from FIFA, this time over the very issue of broken-time payments to Olympic Games competitors, a matter that would rumble on until after World War II.

England's pre-eminence

Even if England had been in the international footballing fold in 1930, it was unlikely to have been interested in participating in the inaugural World Cup. The country that had given football to the world still believed in its pre-eminence. There may have been the odd defeat by the other home countries, but England had no need to prove itself against overseas opposition. A 4–3 defeat against Spain in Madrid in May 1929 was England's first loss to a foreign side, and even that was avenged with a 7–1 thumping at Highbury two years later.

While the Home Countries stood on the sidelines, the World Cup party got underway. Hosts Uruguay were the inaugural winners, an early indication that home advantage gave a huge boost to a country's chances. In the final, staged at the new Centenario Stadium, Uruguay came from behind to beat arch-rivals Argentina 4–2. The two camps couldn't even agree which ball to

World Cup Final 1966
When football came home

Relying on the team which had seen them through the previous two rounds, Alf Ramsey's England won a great match 4–2 after extra-time against West Germany.

The Germans had looked the more dangerous in the opening minutes, Haller and Held leading menacing sorties and Seeler, their captain, using his head to good advantage.

It came as no surprise when Haller shot West Germany into a 12th-minute lead following Wilson's misdirected header. He thought scoring the opening goal entitled him to keep the match ball – that was the custom in German football.

England, behind for the first time in the tournament, equalised six minutes later. Hurst positioned himself perfectly to head home Moore's quickly-taken free kick.

The German defence gave little away in the second period and only 12 minutes remained when Peters scored after Hurst's shot had struck a defender and looped invitingly into the air. From that range Peters could hardly miss.

As England hung on for the final whistle, Jack Charlton was adjudged, harshly, to have fouled on the edge of the box. The free kick, blasted at the wall by Emmerich, appeared to strike Schnellinger's hand before rolling on for Weber to shoot, almost in slow motion, past Banks' desperate lunge.

England looked fitter and fresher in extra time, continuing to play with confidence and composure. Hurst scored with a drive on the turn which hit the underside of the bar and bounced over the line with Tilkowski beaten. The goal was disputed by the Germans – and still is. The Swiss referee asked the nearer linesman, Mr Bakhramov from the USSR (he actually came from what is now Azerbaijan), and between them they agreed that it was a goal.

With the last kick of the match Hurst completed a personal triumph by scoring with a firm left-footer. There were some people on the pitch.

Geoff, now Sir Geoff, remains the only player to have notched a hat-trick in a World Cup Final.

Final
England v West Germany 4–2*

HALF TIME 1–1, 90 MIN 2–2, * AFTER EXTRA TIME
ATTENDANCE 96,924
SCORERS
ENGLAND: HURST 3, PETERS
W.GERMANY: HALLER, WEBER

England	W.Germany
BANKS	TILKOWSKI
COHEN	HÖTTGES
WILSON	SCHNELLINGER
STILES	BECKENBAUER
J.CHARLTON	SCHÜLZ
MOORE	WEBER
BALL	HALLER
HUNT	OVERATH
R.CHARLTON	SEELER
HURST	HELD
PETERS	EMMERICH

use for the game. It is said that each provided a ball for 45 minutes, the original 'game of two halves'.

Since that Uruguayan victory, five more tournaments have been won by the country staging the finals. The percentage increases still further if it is extended to the continent hosting the event, rather than the individual country. If the Americas are taken as an entity, only Brazil has triumphed outside its continental boundaries, in Sweden in 1958, and in Japan and Korea four years ago.

Only seven winning countries

Brazil's five wins make it the most successful nation in World Cup history. It is also the only country to have contested every final to date. Italy and West Germany come second in the all-time list with three wins apiece. West Germany's last success, at Italia '90, came just prior to reunification. Uruguay and Argentina are the only other countries to have held the trophy aloft more than once, with England '66 and France '98 rounding out the roll of honour. Thus, only seven countries have lifted the trophy in its 76-year history.

When Pele-inspired Brazil completed its hat-trick, in Mexico in 1970, it won the original Jules Rimet trophy outright. West Germany's Franz Beckenbauer became the first man to lift the new trophy, in 1974. The winners actually receive replicas; FIFA jealously guards the original – unsurprisingly, as the Jules Rimet trophy was famously stolen while on display in the run-up to the 1966 finals in England. Pickles the dog saved the day, unearthing the gold statue in a South London garden to take his place in football's lexicon.

After Sweden '58, it was decided that the finals would alternate between Europe and the Americas. That arrangement prevailed for the next 44 years, until Japan and Korea co-hosted the 2002 tournament. South Africa will stage the 2010 jamboree, leaving Oceania the only FIFA-affiliated confederation not to have played host. No doubt its day will come.

Changes in format

The World Cup has undergone numerous changes in format. After the invitation-only inaugural event, qualification arrived in 1934, a 32-strong entry being whittled down to 16 for the finals in Italy. That tournament, and its successor in France, was run on a straight knockout basis. This meant that some countries circumnavigated the globe to play a single match. Brazil and Argentina, both first-round losers in 1934, suffered just such a fate. Holders Uruguay didn't; that country declined to enter in tit-for-tat retaliation for Europe's lack of representation in 1930. The greatest festival of football on the planet has not been immune from political points-scoring.

Group matches were restored for Brazil 1950, the first post-war competiton, when the Home Countries deigned to enter for the first time. England qualified by winning the Home International Championship – then failed to progress beyond the group stage after going down 1–0 to USA in Belo Horizonte. The standard of football in America was nothing like it is today, and David's slaying of Goliath was of such an order of magnitude that one press agency, convinced that the result had been transmitted in error,

Left: Brazil captain Cafu holds the trophy in 2002.

gave the score out as a much more believable 10–1 victory to England. Matthews, Finney and co. at least made it to Brazil. Scotland, who finished second in the domestic championship, was also offered a place but declined, the SFA declaring it would only enter the World Cup as winners of the Home International tournament.

No showpiece final

The return of group matches in 1950 was a much more sensible format – except for the fact that the organisers bizarrely decided that a showpiece final was an unnecessary appendage. The winners of the round-robin second group phase would be the world champions. Fortunately, the final match pitted Uruguay against Brazil, the two contenders for the crown, so the competition did get a final via the back door. Uruguay won 2–1 to lift the trophy for the second time, emulating Italy's feat of the 1930s.

A 16-nation tournament, with the top two in each group proceeding to the knockout stage, prevailed until 1974, when FIFA reintroduced a second-round group phase. Eight years later, the increasing breadth and depth of the game across the globe prompted FIFA to expand the finals to a 24-team entry. Mexico '86 saw the return of a straight knockout when teams reached the last 16. Unfortunately, to make up that number it meant that in four of the six first-round groups, three teams went through. In other words, the first 36 matches of the tournament eliminated just eight of the 24 teams. That anomaly disappeared at France '98, when the tournament was further expanded to 32 teams, with the top two in each of the eight groups going forward to the knockout stage.

From its embryonic beginnings over a century ago, the World Cup has grown into a dazzling media event, a multi-billion dollar festival. Much more importantly, it is a four-yearly party where the world game struts its stuff and everyone is invited.

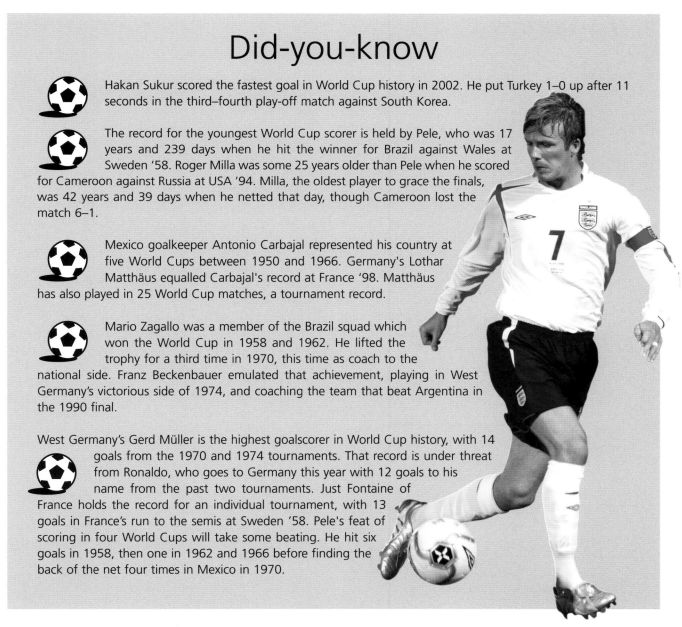

Did-you-know

Hakan Sukur scored the fastest goal in World Cup history in 2002. He put Turkey 1–0 up after 11 seconds in the third–fourth play-off match against South Korea.

The record for the youngest World Cup scorer is held by Pele, who was 17 years and 239 days when he hit the winner for Brazil against Wales at Sweden '58. Roger Milla was some 25 years older than Pele when he scored for Cameroon against Russia at USA '94. Milla, the oldest player to grace the finals, was 42 years and 39 days when he netted that day, though Cameroon lost the match 6–1.

Mexico goalkeeper Antonio Carbajal represented his country at five World Cups between 1950 and 1966. Germany's Lothar Matthäus equalled Carbajal's record at France '98. Matthäus has also played in 25 World Cup matches, a tournament record.

Mario Zagallo was a member of the Brazil squad which won the World Cup in 1958 and 1962. He lifted the trophy for a third time in 1970, this time as coach to the national side. Franz Beckenbauer emulated that achievement, playing in West Germany's victorious side of 1974, and coaching the team that beat Argentina in the 1990 final.

West Germany's Gerd Müller is the highest goalscorer in World Cup history, with 14 goals from the 1970 and 1974 tournaments. That record is under threat from Ronaldo, who goes to Germany this year with 12 goals to his name from the past two tournaments. Just Fontaine of France holds the record for an individual tournament, with 13 goals in France's run to the semis at Sweden '58. Pele's feat of scoring in four World Cups will take some beating. He hit six goals in 1958, then one in 1962 and 1966 before finding the back of the net four times in Mexico in 1970.

World Cup 2006 Planner

GROUP A

	P	W	L	D	F	A	PTS
1							
2							
3							
4							

JUN 9	MUNICH	GERMANY	V	COSTA RICA	__:__
JUN 9	GELSENKIRCHEN	POLAND	V	ECUADOR	__:__
JUN 14	DORTMUND	GERMANY	V	POLAND	__:__
JUN 15	HAMBURG	ECUADOR	V	COSTA RICA	__:__
JUN 20	BERLIN	ECUADOR	V	GERMANY	__:__
JUN 20	HANOVER	COSTA RICA	V	POLAND	__:__

GROUP B

	P	W	L	D	F	A	PTS
1							
2							
3							
4							

JUN 10	FRANKFURT	ENGLAND	V	PARAGUAY	__:__
JUN 10	DORTMUND	TRINIDAD&T	V	SWEDEN	__:__
JUN 15	NUREMBERG	ENGLAND	V	TRINIDAD&T	__:__
JUN 15	BERLIN	SWEDEN	V	PARAGUAY	__:__
JUN 20	COLOGNE	SWEDEN	V	ENGLAND	__:__
JUN 20	KAISERSLAUTERN	PARAGUAY	V	TRINIDAD&T	__:__

GROUP C

	P	W	L	D	F	A	PTS
1							
2							
3							
4							

JUN 10	HAMBURG	IVORY COAST	V	ARGENTINA	__:__
JUN 11	LEIPZIG	SERBIA&M	V	HOLLAND	__:__
JUN 16	GELSENKIRCHEN	ARGENTINA	V	SERBIA&M	__:__
JUN 16	STUTTGART	IVORY COAST	V	HOLLAND	__:__
JUN 21	FRANKFURT	HOLLAND	V	ARGENTINA	__:__
JUN 21	MUNICH	IVORY COAST	V	SERBIA&M	__:__

GROUP D

	P	W	L	D	F	A	PTS
1							
2							
3							
4							

JUN 11	NUREMBERG	MEXICO	V	IRAN	__:__
JUN 11	COLOGNE	ANGOLA	V	PORTUGAL	__:__
JUN 16	HANOVER	MEXICO	V	ANGOLA	__:__
JUN 17	FRANKFURT	PORTUGAL	V	IRAN	__:__
JUN 21	GELSENKIRCHEN	PORTUGAL	V	MEXICO	__:__
JUN 21	LEIPZIG	IRAN	V	ANGOLA	__:__

GROUP E

	P	W	L	D	F	A	PTS
1							
2							
3							
4							

JUN 12	HANOVER	ITALY	V	GHANA	__:__
JUN 12	GELSENKIRCHEN	USA	V	CZECH REP	__:__
JUN 17	KAISERSLAUTERN	ITALY	V	USA	__:__
JUN 17	COLOGNE	CZECH REP	V	GHANA	__:__
JUN 22	HAMBURG	CZECH REP	V	ITALY	__:__
JUN 22	NUREMBERG	GHANA	V	USA	__:__

GROUP F

	P	W	L	D	F	A	PTS
1							
2							
3							
4							

JUN 12	KAISERSLAUTERN	AUSTRALIA	V	JAPAN	__:__
JUN 13	BERLIN	BRAZIL	V	CROATIA	__:__
JUN 18	NUREMBERG	JAPAN	V	CROATIA	__:__
JUN 18	MUNICH	BRAZIL	V	AUSTRALIA	__:__
JUN 22	DORTMUND	JAPAN	V	BRAZIL	__:__
JUN 22	STUTTGART	CROATIA	V	AUSTRALIA	__:__

GROUP G

	P	W	L	D	F	A	PTS
1							
2							
3							
4							

JUN 13	FRANKFURT	S KOREA	V	TOGO	__:__
JUN 13	STUTTGART	SWITZERLAND	V	FRANCE	__:__
JUN 18	LEIPZIG	FRANCE	V	S KOREA	__:__
JUN 19	DORTMUND	SWITZERLAND	V	TOGO	__:__
JUN 23	COLOGNE	TOGO	V	FRANCE	__:__
JUN 23	HANOVER	SWITZERLAND	V	S KOREA	__:__

GROUP H

	P	W	L	D	F	A	PTS
1							
2							
3							
4							

JUN 14	LEIPZIG	SPAIN	V	UKRAINE	__:__
JUN 14	MUNICH	SAUDI ARABIA	V	TUNISIA	__:__
JUN 19	HAMBURG	SAUDI ARABIA	V	UKRAINE	__:__
JUN 19	STUTTGART	SPAIN	V	TUNISIA	__:__
JUN 23	KAISERSLAUTERN	SAUDI ARABIA	V	SPAIN	__:__
JUN 23	BERLIN	UKRAINE	V	TUNISIA	__:__

2nd Round

MATCH 1
(WINNER A) _____ V (RUNNER-UP B) _____ : _____
24 JUN MUNICH

MATCH 2
(WINNER C) _____ V (RUNNER-UP D) _____ : _____
24 JUN LEIPZIG

MATCH 3
(WINNER B) _____ V (RUNNER-UP A) _____ : _____
25 JUN STUTTGART

MATCH 4
(WINNER D) _____ V (RUNNER-UP C) _____ : _____
25 JUN NUREMBERG

MATCH 5
(WINNER E) _____ V (RUNNER-UP F) _____ : _____
26 JUN KAISERSLAUTERN

MATCH 6
(WINNER G) _____ V (RUNNER-UP H) _____ : _____
26 JUN COLOGNE

MATCH 7
(WINNER F) _____ V (RUNNER-UP E) _____ : _____
27 JUN DORTMUND

MATCH 8
(WINNER H) _____ V (RUNNER-UP G) _____ : _____
27 JUN HANOVER

Quarter Finals

MATCH A
(WINNER 1) _____ V (WINNER 2) _____ : _____
30 JUN BERLIN

MATCH B
(WINNER 5) _____ V (WINNER 6) _____ : _____
30 JUN HAMBURG

MATCH C
(WINNER 3) _____ V (WINNER 4) _____ : _____
01 JUL GELSENKIRCHEN

MATCH D
(WINNER 7) _____ V (WINNER 8) _____ : _____
01 JUL FRANKFURT

Semi Finals

SF I
(WINNER QF A) _____ V (WINNER QF B) _____ : _____
04 JUL DORTMUND

SF II
(WINNER QF C) _____ V (WINNER QF D) _____ : _____
05 JUL MUNICH

Third Place

8PM
(LOSER SF I) _____ V (LOSER SF II) _____ : _____
08 JUL STUTTGART

Final

(WINNER SF I) _____ V (WINNER SF II) _____ : _____
09 JUL BERLIN

2006 World Champions _____

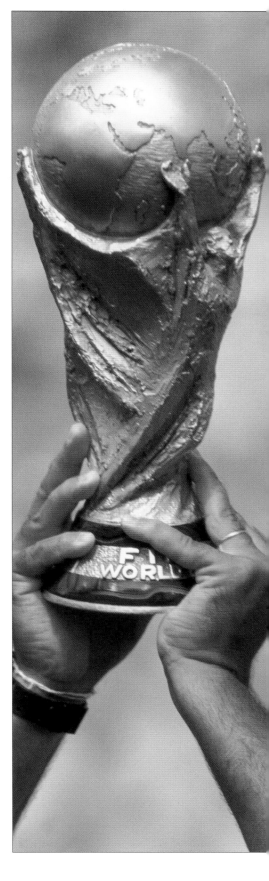

Acknowledgements

Particular thanks to
Tom Whiting, Kate Truman, Simon Taylor, Sarah Rickayzen
Design by John Dunne